*Jane and
Her Gentlemen*

AUDREY HAWKRIDGE

Jane and Her Gentlemen

Jane Austen
and the Men in Her Life
and Novels

PETER OWEN PUBLISHERS

London & Chester Springs

PETER OWEN PUBLISHERS
73 Kenway Road, London SW5 0RE

Peter Owen books are distributed in the USA by Dufour Editions Inc.,
Chester Springs, PA 19425-0007

First published in Great Britain 2000
© Audrey Hawkridge 2000

ISBN 0 7206 1104 0

A catalogue record for this book is available from the British Library.

Printed in Great Britain by MPG Books Ltd, Bodmin, Cornwall

Acknowledgements

My grateful thanks are extended to Jean Bowden, archivist and retired curator of Jane Austen's House, Chawton, for the many years of her expert guidance and encouragement; the Jane Austen Memorial Trust and its chairman Tom Carpenter; the Jane Austen Society, particularly Brian Southam and Helen Lefroy; Hampshire Record Office and my very capable friends there; the Mary Evans Picture Library; and Henrietta Hellard, for her list of rectors on display in Cheriton Church, Hampshire. I also sincerely appreciate the generous assistance and most useful information given to me by Joan Austen-Leigh, Henry Rice and the late Diana Kleyn, as well as the kindness I have received from the owners of pictures in private collections, who have so readily made these available to me. I have been greatly assisted in this undertaking by Deirdre Le Faye's comprehensive and informative edition of Jane Austen's letters. In addition, I should like to thank the many helpful people who tried, sadly without success, to trace for me the James Northcote portrait of Samuel Blackall.

To my editors at Peter Owen, Antonia Owen and Simon Smith, I am very much indebted for their valuable advice and hard work on my behalf, as well as to Keith Savage for his important contribution to this book as its designer.

I am also grateful for permission to quote from the following publications: *Collected Reports of the Jane Austen Society, 1976–1985* and *My Aunt Jane Austen* by Caroline Austen, the Jane Austen Society; *Jane Austen* by Elizabeth Jenkins, reproduced with permission of Curtis Brown, London, on behalf of © Elizabeth Jenkins, 1938, 1972; *Jane Austen's Family Through Five Generations* by Maggie Lane, Robert Hale, London; *Jane Austen: A Character Study* by Margaret Llewelyn, HarperCollins, London; *Jane Austen in Kent* by David Waldron Smithers, Hurtwood Press, Westerham; extracts reprinted from *Jane Austen, Facts and Problems* by R.W. Chapman (1948) and *Jane Austen and Her Art* by Mary Lascelles (1939), both Clarendon Press, by permission of Oxford University Press, Oxford; extracts reprinted from *Jane Austen's Letters*, collected and edited by Deirdre Le Faye (3rd edition, 1995), © Deirdre Le Faye, 1995, by permission of Oxford University Press, Oxford; *The Diary of Sir Walter Scott, 1825-32*, the Pierpont Morgan Library, New York, MA441-42; *Transactions of the Royal Society of Literature, Essays by Divers Hands, VIII*, 1928, the Royal Society of Literature, London; and *Jane Austen's Literary Manuscripts* by B.C. Southam, with the kind permission of the author.

And, finally, I must thank my dear husband for his very practical support, given cheerfully and unstintingly at all times.

Foreword

Trying to write something fresh about Jane Austen is like tiptoeing through a ploughed field in the hope of finding virgin soil, only to discover that much of the earth has already been turned. Nearly every conclusion drawn proves to have been published before – so that to delve further can seem almost impertinent. Yet her readers never give up expecting to find new angles from which to view her and, from these, new ways in which to examine her. If in attempting to do this I have made 'original' observations that are in fact far from new, I apologize in advance. And an apology may also seem due for the recital of well-known biographical details or facets of character which familiarity makes tedious; but background is important, and to presuppose the reader's knowledge is unfair to those who know Jane only through her novels or their filmed versions.

This particular examination of Jane's world looks at the men in her family and her social circle, what she thought of them and how they affected her life. They cast their own light on the men in her works, most of whom she presents so roundly that we feel they are old friends, to admire or smile at as she intended but never to hate. Her way of thinking and writing is moderate and tolerant. It is much closer in spirit to the best precepts of the late twentieth century than to the Victorians following her who stifled themselves under the weight of their own heavy moralizing but whose fictional flow, by contrast, tended to regress to Gothic melodrama as ludicrous in Jane's eyes as in ours.

The men of Jane's novels, for the most part, must mainly be the children of her invention; but fiction being a blend of imagination and experience, her male creations cannot help owing something to the real men in her life. And, though we have long since discarded their measured speech and formal manners, many of them are men whom we encounter daily in our own lives, too.

In the quotations from the letters of Jane and her contemporaries, I have adhered where possible to the original spelling and abbreviations – as well as some occasional and unusual linking of words. However, a little of her more unorthodox punctuation has been removed for the sake of smoother reading and clarity.

Contents

List of Illustrations   10

Part I: Jane

1 From Steventon to Chawton   15

2 Conflicting Characteristics   33

Part II: The Men at Home

3 In Hampshire and Kent   51

4 'Not a Mind for Affliction'   65

5 The Admirals   79

Part III: Cameos

6 Gentlemen Observed   99

7 'Giving Universal Pleasure'   111

8 Anti-Heroes   127

Part IV: Romance in Fiction and Fact

9 Husbands for Heroines   139

10 In Search of Love   151

11 Retraction and Refusal   169

Notes   187

Select Bibliography   193

Appendix 1: A Brief Chronology of Jane Austen's Life   195

Appendix 2: The Austen Family Tree   196

Index   199

List of Illustrations

between pages 110 and 111

1 The Reverend George Austen

2 Mrs George Austen

3 Cassandra Austen

4 The Reverend James Austen

5 Edward (Austen) Knight

6 The Reverend Henry Austen

7 Admiral of the Fleet Sir Francis (Frank) Austen

8 Rear-Admiral Charles Austen

9 Martha Lloyd, later Lady Austen

10 The Reverend James Edward Austen-Leigh

11 Steventon Rectory, Hampshire

12 Godmersham Park, Kent

13 Chawton Great House, Hampshire

14 Jane Austen's house, Chawton, Hampshire as it looked in her day

15 Jane Austen's house as it looks today (front view)

16 Jane Austen's house as it looks today (side view)

17 The table on which Jane wrote her novels

18 The bedroom Jane shared with her sister Cassandra

19 Two topaz crosses given to Jane and Cassandra by their brother Charles

20 A list of rectors in Cheriton Church, near Alresford, Hampshire

21 Thomas Langlois Lefroy

22 Harris Bigg-Wither

23 Manydown Park, Hampshire

24 The Rice Portrait, believed to be of Jane

'I am too proud of my gentlemen to admit that
they were only Mr A or Colonel B.'

– Jane Austen

PART I

Jane

1

From Steventon to Chawton

TO generations of readers Jane Austen once seemed the definitive female of her time. The tradition of eighteenth-century womanhood, totally wrapped up in the eternal hunt for 'a single man in possession of a good fortune', requires a figurehead to epitomize it, and Jane was frequently cast in that role, which appears at first glance to suit her. But, first glances being unreliable, people have in recent years been looking at her through very different eyes.

In some ways she may indeed have been typical of the old middle-class country parson's daughter, albeit with a dash of spice in her Regency thinking and speech which sent a refined shudder through the frame of at least one of her Victorian nieces. However, where men and marriage were concerned, most modern studies of Jane accept that she held quite avant-garde views of a firmly independent calibre; she was a feminist ahead of her time.

But her early and barely recognizable essay in feminism was of an altogether milder variety than our contemporary interpretation of the word, which occasionally suggests deep-seated resentment of men in general. She longed for the crushing wrongs against women to be righted, but her wildest hopes for female enfranchisement must have stopped there. Powerless as she was, even wielding her pen in ladylike anonymity, there was nothing she would have felt she could do beyond theorizing. As for the germ of practical feminism in her nature, it was so inextricably bound up with the opposing force of her femininity, her interest in the male sex and the time-honoured desire to make herself attractive, that it might have been permanently put to rest if a sufficiently scintillating man had come into her life to stay. There were many men whom she liked or loved, and, while deploring injustice outside her own home, she was such a cheerful and willing handmaiden to the men in her family that she would driven any feminist of today to despair.

Until fairly recently, women had to rely entirely on men for their status and comforts, so that they would have always expected to try to marry if they possibly could. And this was the area in which Jane subscribed to an opinion two centuries in advance of her time: that marriage merely as an end in itself – with all its attendant woes of dutiful companionship, perhaps in the face of soul-destroying incompatibility or of chronic ill health from constant childbearing – was a risk to be avoided. Such a revolutionary thesis could not be expounded outright in her novels – for the moment was by no means ripe for female individualism to creep into romantic literature – but she made her feelings clear in the way she chose to shape her life.

Most of Jane's women friends, like the women she created in fiction, must have been heavily preoccupied with the vital necessity of finding men willing and able to rescue them from an old age where they would either struggle to make ends meet or else live in grateful dependence on male relatives who had prior commitments of their own. The often frenetic nature of this searching was understandable, for there were not too many years in which a woman was eligible for a first marriage. She could as a rule expect to find her mate only when she was between the ages of about sixteen and twenty-six, with her wealth, health, pedigree and appearance influencing the range of choice, much as it has always done in the bloodstock markets of the world. So speed was important, yet difficult to achieve in the slow pace at which life moved then.

The task was made more complicated since custom dictated that the quarry should be coerced into believing he was the hunter, and during his stately courtship there should be as little overt encouragement of his attentions as possible. Whether this was more frustrating to the male or the female of the species is any-body's guess. But our image of well-bred courtship at the time is of the meek quiescent girl chaperoned to one drawing-room after another for inspection by mothers of suitable bachelors or, for light relief, battling her way with a clutch of hopeful sisters through the squash of an assembly hall – not to find as her dancing partner some divine stranger who has spotted her across a crowded room but, instead, someone safe who has secured an introduction to her through a respectable third party.

However, Jane herself was no crushed mouse dutifully parading in the marriage sale-room. While she enjoyed cavorting at Basingstoke balls with as many different partners as etiquette and the clock would allow, she stopped short of the final requirements, which were to marry where prudence dictated and subordinate her personality for the rest of her days in a loveless match. For a lifetime with the right man she might cheerfully have given up her independence, but that chance was denied her. She did, of course, provide all her fortunate heroines with husbands whom they considered the right men (even if we would disagree with one or two of them) once they had first gone through the statutory tribulations of the romantic novel format. But outside the realm of fiction, her own critical and discerning mind shook off the dread of spinsterhood that paralysed most of the women of her own world in a way that she could not allow her heroines to do – apart from Emma Woodhouse, who did not expect to marry and whose wealth would in due time have brought emancipation. Though well aware that it was not the path to prosperity, Jane knew that a future spent with a well-loved sister and their gently hypochondriac mother on an income of £210 per annum – supplemented by better-off brothers – was far more promising than life with the wrong husband. So Jane settled for single blessedness, if not joyously at least contentedly.

The fact that she dwelt for eight years in a 'cottage' (with five main bedrooms and a third storey for a servant!), as well as lacking a horse and carriage of her own to drive, is occasionally taken to mean that she had little experience of the county social whirl or of elegant ladies and gentlemen to match the characters in her books. She is even pictured sometimes as a sharp, waspish woman looking at life out of a lonely window, envy leaking through the delicate film of her well-phrased, rather cynical wit. This is far from the truth. Cynical she may have been, like most close observers of human behaviour. But she moved with social ease in great houses, among well-to-do relatives, in-laws and friends; she travelled frequently, and extensively, if we make due allowance for the poor roads of the time; and two weeks before her twenty-seventh birthday she had a proposal of marriage from a young heir to fifteen hundred acres and a handsome mansion, set in lush surroundings which not even the mightiest of Lady Catherines would have dismissed as 'a very small park'.[1]

*

While looking at Jane and her gentlemen it is necessary to glance at her background as well as at the kind of person she was. She first saw the light of day on 16 December 1775 at Steventon Rectory, eight miles south-west of Basingstoke in Hampshire, where her father George Austen was the incumbent. The Austens had eight children: James (1765–1819); George, who suffered from severe epilepsy and was reared by another family who could give him full-time attention and thus never figures in the family records (1766–1838); Edward (1767–1852); Henry (1771–1850); Cassandra, named after her mother, formerly Miss Cassandra Leigh (1773–1845); Francis, known as Frank (1774–1865); Jane (1775–1817); and Charles (1779–1852). Two of these boys grew up to follow their father into the Church and two to attain high rank in the Navy. And one, with great good luck, became a wealthy landowner.

Mr and Mrs Austen sprang from equally prosperous families, though neither of them had a surplus of money themselves. The Austens originated in Kent, and because of his father's early death Mr Austen was dependent for the living of Steventon on a rich cousin, Thomas Knight – who owned a great deal of Hampshire land but lived in splendour at Godmersham Park, near Faversham, Kent – and dependent for the living of nearby Deane, to which he was also appointed, on his uncle Francis Austen of the Red House, Sevenoaks, also in Kent. His wife, related to the Duke of Chandos, was descended from the Leighs of Stoneleigh Abbey, Warwickshire, a massive pile with forty-five windows in front, its own chapel and over four acres of kitchen garden alone. But she was destined permanently to be the poor relation. When he died, her rich brother James Leigh Perrot, after whom she had hopefully named her first-born, shocked the family by excluding her, his only surviving sister and needy to boot, from his will. However, though she was not lucky in legacies, she seems to have been lucky enough in love, and the Austens were happy both with each other and with their children.

The Parsonage House, as it was called by the villagers,[2] was pulled down by Jane's nephew William Knight, a later rector. But when she lived there it was a comfortable home, two-storeyed in addition to its attics, with a carriage drive on one side and a garden on the other, a grassy terrace, hedgerows, shrubberies and graceful elms – some of the latter being eventually picked off, while Jane watched, by one of the fierce great winds which smote southern England during the eighteenth century.[3] There was also a dairy with five cows and, beside the house, a large barn dry and warm enough to serve for overflow entertainment. The rural picture was completed by a nearby street of cottages.

Mr Austen took in resident – and often aristocratic – pupils, educating his own boys alongside them. For a short while Cassandra and Jane went to cosy, moderately academic boarding-schools for girls at Oxford and Reading Abbey but, like their brothers, much of their knowledge was imbibed at home. Jane learned French, Italian, music (pianoforte and singing) and was very expert with her needle. Work was no hardship and her childhood was a pleasant one.

Descriptions of her as an adult have been left behind by Austens of two generations. Her favourite brother Henry spoke of her after she died with a gravity natural under the circumstances but foreign to his sparkling nature. Her stature, he said, was elegant and of a perfect height, and she carried herself with quiet grace. She had good features, a cheerful and benevolent expression, her conversation was excellent yet kind and 'she always sought in the faults of others something to excuse, forgive or forget. She never uttered a hasty, a silly, or a severe expression.'[4]

This, being a considered eulogy, would certainly never have contained adverse criticism; nor could anyone expect it to do so. And the understanding between Jane and Henry was so finely tuned that he probably never noticed the weaknesses which in any case loyalty would have forbidden him to acknowledge. Perhaps the comments from a niece and nephew, children of her brother James, are worth more, by virtue of distance, than those of a fond brother. Jane's was apparently the first face that young Caroline Austen remembered thinking pretty – the child's mother was plain and pockmarked, unfortunately. It was a rounded face, she wrote, with 'a clear brown complexion and very good hazle eyes . . . Her hair, a darkish brown, curled naturally – it was in short curls round her face.'[5] Of her aunt's disposition she said, in defence, it seems, against sniping by early critics:

> my Aunt Jane had a regard for her neighbours and felt a kindly interest in their proceedings . . . They sometimes served for her amusement, but it was her own nonsense that gave zest to the gossip – She never turned *them* into ridicule – She was as far as possible from being either censorious or satirical.[6]

Her nephew James Edward Austen-Leigh, Caroline's brother, also left a description frequently quoted: 'If not so regularly hand-some as her sister, yet her countenance had a peculiar charm of its own to the eyes of most beholders.'[7] But he deplored her habit of wearing a cap all day, feeling that both Jane and Cassandra could have paid more attention to fashion and not worn middle-aged clothes before their time. He could not be expected to have known, however, that caps were easier to manage and cheaper to arrange than dressed hair. But Jane at least was coaxed out of hers once in London, in her late thirties, being 'curled . . . out at a great rate' by a hairdresser important enough to be referred to as Mr Hall. 'I thought it looked hideous,' she reported, 'and longed for a snug cap instead, but my companions silenced me by their admir-ation. I had only a bit of velvet round my head.'[8]

Her nephew and niece naturally did not see her at her best. As a young woman she had clearly been very attractive. By the time she had begun to be called Jane, instead of the childhood 'Jenny', she was still carrying a little puppy fat on her face, though it had fallen off elsewhere. But before long her face had fined down too, so that her cousin (and, later, sister-in-law) Eliza wrote from afar that she had heard of Jane and Cassandra's success with men and concluded that they must be among the prettiest girls in England.[9] Eliza did tend to overstate the case in her descriptions, especially when rhapsodizing about her own success with men; however, here, with great generosity, she was being highly complimentary to two other women. It was not all idle flattery. Jane and Cassandra certainly were popular girls, and Jane particularly was in her element when dancing – a pastime at which she excelled. Her neat handwriting, excellent needlework and orderly habits may suggest a home-bird but, despite these and her quiet elegance, there was nothing of the retiring *hausfrau* about Jane as a young woman. On the contrary, she was determinedly outgoing, using to the full her vivacity, sense of humour and attractive speaking voice to flirt her way from one Hampshire party to another.

Not everyone, of course, likes vivacious, laughing flirts. E.M. Forster, gazing down from the remote tower of his bachelor world and knowing nothing about girlish conversations or sisterly chit-chat, likened her to her own Lydia Bennet and scorned her youthful preoccupation with, as he put it, 'officers, dances, officers, giggling' in her letters to Cassandra.[10] And the Hampshire author Mary Russell Mitford had a mother who was not at all impressed with Jane's charms, calling her 'the prettiest, silliest, most affected, husband-hunting butterfly' she ever remembered.[11] As Jane's biographer Lord David Cecil points out, the Mitfords had left the Steventon area when Jane was ten, so she was probably speaking on hearsay; however, they moved only to Alresford, about twelve miles away. In any case, it does not alter the judgement. Someone or other said it about Jane, much to the disgust of those of her admirers who find it hard to accept that she was ever immature. But even this showed profits. Many women who end up as wise and circumspect as Elizabeth Bennet, Elinor Dashwood or Anne Elliot start out as giddy as Lydia. If a girl never goes through a first frivolous, husband-hunting butterfly stage herself, how is she able to write with such luscious insight into the characters of other butterflies? And seeming silly would certainly not have operated to her disadvantage. Forty years earlier Lady Mary Wortley-Montagu had exhorted her granddaughter to conceal her learning 'with as much solicitude as she would hide crookedness or lameness'. Accomplishments were desirable in young ladies but scholarly conversation was not. The Georgians lagged far behind their Tudor ancestors, some of whose women read Latin and Greek without incurring universal male disapproval. Eighteenth-century men, however, found intellectual women unnerving and thus unattractive. Jane notes this fact in *Northanger Abbey*:

> A woman . . . if she have the misfortune of knowing anything, should conceal it as well as she can . . . I will only add in justice to men, that though to the larger and more trifling part of the sex, imbecility in females is a great enhancement of their personal charms, there is a portion of them too reasonable and too well-informed themselves to desire anything more in woman than ignorance . . . a good-looking girl, with an affectionate heart and a very ignorant mind, cannot fail of attracting a clever young man, unless circumstances are particularly untoward.[12]

One of her heroes recognized man's need to feel mentally superior to woman. 'Frederick will not be the first man who has chosen a wife with less sense than his family expected,' says Henry Tilney in the same novel, referring to his brother's brief wooing of the shriekingly shallow Isabella Thorpe.[13] The said Frederick is too astute to get permanently ensnared, but Jane was acquainted with a great many men who were far from astute. So, knowing their weaknesses, she exercised the light touch and fluttered around the flower of male Hampshire society without an apparent thought in her head, while silently storing all observations for future use.

*

The social butterfly image which she presented was all the more of an achievement since another of her cousins, Philadelphia Walter, said that as a child of twelve Jane was prim, whimsical and affected – which probably in fact just meant that she was shy. Shyness, or diffidence, remained, paradoxically, part of her make-up. When her father tried to get *Pride and Prejudice* published for her in November 1797 (under its original title *First Impressions*), his selected publisher, Cadell, declined to take a look. Some writers are buoyed up by the conviction that they have a great masterpiece to give to the world; Jane was not. Feeling on unsure ground, she meekly put the manuscript away, to be revised some years later.

And she was shy in ways other than in the mere acceptance of defeat before battle had even commenced. Outside her immediate circle, the letters she wrote were couched in a rather aloof style, compatible with the formality of her era but not typical of her delivery for home consumption. The Austens in their dealings with outsiders were emotionally restrained and unsentimental. They were dignified in their sorrows and did their laughing together in private. However, surprisingly for such a reserved group of people, they enjoyed acting – most of them. The Steventon Rectory barn was set aside for amateur theatricals, and all the family were encouraged by Mrs Austen to take part, behind the scenes if not at centre stage.

The star player seems to have been Cousin Eliza, daughter of Mr Austen's sister Mrs Philadelphia Hancock. Eliza had married a French aristocrat, the Comte de Feuillide. She came to England for the birth of her son Hastings (named after her godfather Warren Hastings) in 1786, and then again under sadder circumstances in 1794 after her husband was guillotined in a tragic attempt to help a friend. On the first visit Eliza played the feminine leads while Jane's brother James wrote the prologues, tackling tragedy and comedy with equal aplomb. Later, during the period when Eliza was widowed and James had lost his first wife, James proposed marriage to Eliza but was refused, so any performances given at that point were no doubt fraught with a few of the undercurrents that Jane provided for the players in *Mansfield Park*. However, James's rival brother Henry (who subsequently did marry Eliza) had not yet entered the lists, being fleetingly engaged to a Miss Pearson.

Jane seems briefly identifiable here with her shy *Mansfield Park* heroine, Fanny Price, who watched with tortured disapproval while the rest of the family made fools of themselves at their domestic theatricals. Jane's own milieu was, after all, on paper and not on the boards. The revulsion that she created in Fanny Price's heart against making a public spectacle of herself before an audience was perhaps the only way she could express her own secret feelings about it, so much at odds – just like Fanny – with the rest of the family. Fanny's hyper-virtuous dislike of a romantic play being enacted at all while the master of the house was away overseas is rather unconvincing, even with the contemporary upsurge of Methodism to serve as an excuse. Surely there had to be something else buried inside Jane to imbue her heroine, for whom she wishes us to feel sympathy, with such palpably priggish rectitude. Jane's pleasures were on the whole quiet ones, except for her beloved dancing and sea-bathing, which she tried out on visits to Lyme and Sidmouth. She read copiously. Fielding and the racier Georgian writers were so familiar to her that, while not choosing their style or their genre for her own novels, she was rendered less self-conscious, and probably less idealistic, about men, life and love than today's readers of her work might suppose; having five virile and much-married brothers helped in this respect, too. She read prose: Addison, Goldsmith, Sheridan and, later, Scott. She admired the works of Samuel Richardson and Samuel Johnson – especially Dr Johnson. And she read poetry under James's guidance, particularly Cowper, for whom she gave Marianne Dashwood a typically fervent admiration in *Sense and Sensibility*. Even more, she loved the poems of the Reverend George Crabbe, even saying she would like to marry him. (A copy of his *Tales* reposed in the *Mansfield Park* Library.)[14] Among the (more rare) women writers, Fanny Burney was fashionable, and Jane read her works too.

Novels of all kinds were appreciated by the family at large – their father being more broadminded than many men of the cloth where literature was concerned – and were often read aloud in the evenings. In most households it would be the men who read while the women sewed, and it must have been the same in the Austen home, for Jane sets scenes like that in nearly all her books. While happy to listen to a well-read story, however, Jane delighted, like many authors, in the golden silence that enables thought to flower and serene companionship that does not require answers to be dredged up out of politeness. 'Our Journey here was perfectly free from accident or Event,' she wrote in 1801; '– we had charming weather, hardly any Dust, & were exceedingly agreable, as we did not speak above once in three miles.'[15]

But the Steventon days of her teens and early twenties were characterized by constant socializing – dining, drinking tea and card-playing among large numbers of people, with a considerable choice of local families. Jane was whisked to weekend house-parties, luncheon-parties, dinner-parties and evening parties – which sometimes went on until three or four in the morning. The hosts were usually friends who would in due course be entertained in return. Occasionally grand dances were held in huge mansions, like those of the Earl of Portsmouth, Lord Dorchester and Lord Bolton. Luckily for the Austen purse, cellar and kitchen-garden, while these gentlemen extended invitations to leading households in the neighbourhood to help swell the throng, they did not expect to be asked back.

In those halcyon days Jane enjoyed all the vigour of healthy youth, revelling in weaving her way through the sets on a crowded ballroom where the couples hardly had space to stand up, and she attended regular assemblies at Basingstoke Town Hall, where on one occasion they found time to squash in twenty dances – not short ones, either. During that period the family owned a carriage, and, if the function they were attending was too far from Steventon, Cassandra and Jane would often stay overnight with their friends Alethea and Catherine Bigg of Manydown Park. With the Napoleonic Wars depriving the county social scene of the Army and Navy, girls found then – as they have done in more recent wars – that if they were really longing to take the floor they might have to partner each other. Jane was no exception. On one occasion she noted that there was 'a scarcity of Men in general, & a still greater scarcity of any that were good for much. – I danced nine dances out of ten, five with Stephen Terry, T. Chute & James Digweed, & four with Catherine.'[16]

Her father decided to retire quite suddenly in 1801, and the family left Steventon to live in Bath. Many young women would have regarded this step as a heaven-sent opportunity for expanding social horizons, but Jane's eyes preferred to rest on peaceful fields and hedgerows, rather than on elegant new streets of creamy Bath stone. However architecturally pleasing town vistas might be – and surely those of Bath in her day were unsurpassed – they never held for her the charm of natural greenery and village lanes. With the well-loved surroundings replaced by scenes and people for whom she felt no great affinity, the social round suddenly palled, and her letters from Bath seem a little out of humour, splashed with vinegar, so to speak. Cassandra and Jane spent much of their time apart, paying long visits to far-off family and friends and writing to each other almost daily. Jane's letters now show her disappointment at the turn life had taken. She attended 'stupid' parties and sat at dull whist-tables,[17] the fault here clearly lying in the company rather than the town. Similarly, when she ventured forth into the lively streets or the quieter hilltops outside the city, she did not seem to be enjoying comfortable strolls with friends but merely enduring boring duty walks with passing acquaintances. By the end of the year, a bustling town dedicated to social pursuits and good health must have suddenly felt more alien still, for it seems that she suffered then the loss of a new friend who in due course might well have become a husband.

The Bath era ended at the beginning of 1805. Her father died, and her mother decided to move back to Hampshire and share the rented Southampton home of Frank Austen, now a naval captain. With the Austen women was their friend Martha Lloyd; her parents had died and her sisters were married – one of them, Mary, to James. From then on she lived with Mrs Austen, Cassandra and Jane as an honorary relative and valued friend. After the first shock of removal, Jane slowly began to see the virtues of visits, cards, walks and company once more. It was a crowded household, a little uncongenial to a writer's soul, but it was a safe harbour and only temporary, for in 1809 she moved to Chawton, near Alton. The four women were all now in a permanent home at last – the bailiff's cottage of the Elizabethan Chawton Great House – where life took on a far more muted tone than it had at Steventon. But the pleasure of being once more an established Hampshire Austen, which always mattered enormously to Jane, made up for any minor privations.

*

Chawton Cottage, dating back to the seventeenth century, is rather larger than its name suggests. It faces the street at the junction of what were then the Gosport, Winchester and London roads. At the meeting point there was once the statutory village pond, gone now like the main highways. Inside, a combined hall and dining-room opened straight on to the street, with a west-facing sitting-room looking out to a large garden with a shrubbery walk. The kitchen and domestic quarters lay behind, with cellars below. Five bedrooms ran off a long passageway above, with attic rooms up a further flight of stairs. Outside there were stables for a donkey and cart and a separate bakehouse – still standing. The village was, unlike most places, a busier place at that time than it is now, with plenty of life going on, which Mrs Austen enjoyed watching from the front windows.

Chawton Great House had by then become the property of Jane's brother Edward. From an early age he was brought up by the childless Thomas Knight, son of their father's benefactor, who planned from the outset to make Edward his heir. After Knight's death, Edward took over Godmersham Park in Kent, Chawton House in Hampshire, a considerable fortune – and, eventually, the

Knight name. This last was not at the time an unusual custom under such circumstances, our ancestors attaching almost more importance to keeping the same surname on the deeds than keeping the same blood in the veins.

Edward Austen, now Knight, was thus able to help out his mother and his sisters in their somewhat straitened circumstances and settle them comfortably in just the kind of situation that would turn out so beneficial to Jane's talents. She had written the first drafts of *Pride and Prejudice*, *Sense and Sensibility* and *Northanger Abbey* while at Steventon. But moving from one temporary home to another had partly stemmed the literary flow for a few years; any kind of domestic upheaval set her back. Cassandra was mainly responsible for the housekeeping – Mrs Austen preferring to restrict her sphere of work to the garden – but when she went to stay in Cheltenham once and left Jane to take over, Jane told her, 'I often wonder how *you* can find time for what you do, in addition to the care of the House . . . Composition seems to me Impossible, with a head full of Joints of Mutton & doses of rhubarb.'[18] This kind of dutiful distraction was understandably more ruinous to the Muse than the pleasurable distractions at Steventon had been.

However, at Chawton, she was dropped by fate into just the right spot to revise the novels she had already written and turn out three more gems: *Mansfield Park*, *Emma* and *Persuasion*. She did her writing in the dining-hall, at a small portable writing-desk and seated near an inner door which conveniently creaked every time it was opened to give warning of anyone's approach. Jane was still in the frustrating stage of having written three novels but with nothing published and was by now naturally a little sensitive about her writing. One or two privileged family members were welcome to look at the finished article but not at the embryo scribbling. Everyone else was kept in the dark, even after publication in some cases. If Jane's attitude were described in the jargon of today, she would probably be called a very private person.

The social butterfly era was dead and gone. But, however Jane behaved, she could never please Mary Russell Mitford, who went now to the other extreme in her criticism and dismissed her as no more regarded in society than a poker or a fire-screen. Apart from visits to stay with her brothers, Jane would indeed to some extent retreat socially during the coming years, but she was to do it a great deal more productively than the scathing Miss Mitford.

From now on the Austen women were cut off from most of their old friends, and they became more self-contained and, by necessity, self-sufficient. Cassandra and Jane wore their dowdy caps and no longer troubled about keeping up with fashion except when they had to visit more elegant establishments. There was not much money to spare to make competitive dressing guilt-free and not much need for competition anyway. The season was ready for the experiences and observations of Jane's lively youth to be transferred to paper, unhampered by too many demands on her time. There was room in the days ahead for old works to be improved and new ones to germinate.

The gentlemen who had led Jane around the Assembly Rooms, ambled beside her in sea-front walking-parties or flirted with her over the coffee cups after dinner were now of the past. In their place arose a new set of gentlemen, the products of her mind. With a foible here and an eccentricity there borrowed from the men who had crowded her life before, and factual background knowledge put to use where necessary, they were created, crafted and polished until they shone gently like antique silver. And then they were sent out to face the world.

2

Conflicting Characteristics

DURING the years before Chawton, Jane's character had gone through the many changes from girlhood to womanhood and displayed some contradictory elements along the way. She has been reproached for coarseness in private correspondence yet praised for delicacy of expression in published works. In some ways she appears snobbish – even allowing for the money- and class-obsessed times in which she lived – and in other ways remarkably liberal in her personal outlook. She is often accused of verbal malice, yet those close to her all saw her as unfailingly kind. Living in a family full of clergymen, she gives away very little of her religious feeling in her books, a fact some people find bewildering. And though there were several juveniles who thought her loving and charming, she seems on the whole to have had a low tolerance level of the very young.

Taking the last first, one has to acknowledge that spoilt children have always been regarded as obnoxious, and there were one or two in her circle whom she could not escape. In her books she creates some infant horrors whose elders cannot or will not control them. They surface in *Sense and Sensibility*, *Persuasion* and *Mansfield Park*. But there is a pleasing little boy in her fragment *The Watsons*, and in *Pride and Prejudice* and *Emma* the children, who are not actually characters with speaking parts, are amiable and well loved, as Jane loved her nieces and nephews. She was on excellent terms with those who were born early enough to remember her.

The eldest, James Edward Austen-Leigh, said that she was the delight of them all: 'We did not think of her as being clever, still less as being famous; but we valued her as one always kind, sympathising, and amusing.'[1] Also, his mother's nephew Fulwar Fowle, recalling Jane from Winchester school-days, told Caroline Austen in 1870 that he remembered Jane as attractive, animated and delightful.[2] And no one could want a better recommendation than Caroline herself gave: 'Her charm to children was great sweetness of manner – she seemed to love you, and you loved her naturally in return –'[3]

With regard to religion, perhaps it was the omnipresence of clergymen in Jane's world – seven of them in the wider reaches of the family and a great many more among their friends – that provides the reason for her lack of comment on the subject. One rarely writes with feeling about something that has, lifelong, been a basic part of the daily round. Admittedly, when Jane wrote about the clergy, she did not please all the real-life members of the profession, Cardinal Newman going so far as to say that she had no romance in her and that her parsons were 'vile creatures'.

She did, however, drag religion rather strangely into one of her letters. While General Sir John Moore was slowly dying on the battlefield of Corunna in January 1809, he said to his second-in-command Colonel Hudson: 'I always wanted to die like this. It is a great satisfaction to know that we have beaten the French. I hope the people of England will be satisfied.' England was satisfied and saddened, too. Jane was merely critical. To her this was of course a topical news item, with great family significance, for her brothers Frank and Charles were then both serving at sea – in fact Frank's ship, the *St Albans*, evacuated some of Sir John's men from Spain. So perhaps her feelings on the subject were confused. In any event, she wrote the following passage to Cassandra, then staying in Kent:

> I am sorry to find that Sir J. Moore has a Mother living, but tho' a very Heroick son, he might not be a very necessary one to her happiness . . . I wish Sir John had united something of the Christian with the Hero in his death.[4]

This is a pitiless judgement on a soldier who kept his stoicism intact to the painful end and who deserved her compassion on that score alone. The last words often attributed to Sir John were 'Remember me to your sister, Stanhope.' They gained fame for their poignant understatement, and one might expect them to have met with Jane's approval – if, that is, she approved of the eccentric Lady Hester Stanhope to whom they referred. Probably she did not; or maybe she subscribed to the view that it was *de rigueur* for great men to die with their Maker's name on their lips and that Sir John failed this test by dreaming of national acclaim and devoting his last thoughts to a woman. No doubt Nelson's pious 'Thank God I have done my duty', uttered just over three years earlier, still rang sonorously in everyone's ears, including Jane's.

This streak of uncharitable callousness, thin though it is, provides fodder for the kind of self-appointed inquisitor who calls her personal correspondence 'a desert of trivialities punctuated by occasional oases of clever malice'.[5] While it is unreasonable to expect private letters, thus vulnerably exposed, never to contain unkind remarks, there are limits which Jane occasionally over-reached, such as her verdict on Richard Waller of Southampton, harsher and balder than the statement on Sir John Moore: 'Mr

Waller is dead, I see; – I cannot greive about it, nor perhaps can his Widow very much.'[6] Most notorious of all is her throwaway line written to Cassandra in 1798 when she was twenty-two: 'Mrs Hall of Sherbourn was brought to bed yesterday of a dead child, some weeks before she expected, oweing to a fright. – I suppose she happened unawares to look at her husband.'[7] The first reaction to this could be to laugh; but the second would surely be to wince, and one can see why Harold Nicolson said she had a mind akin to a small, sharp pair of scissors.[8] In this instance her case has to rest on two small points of defence: her youthful thoughtlessness and our acceptance of eighteenth-century stillbirth as very commonplace. Even so, catty jibes about bereavement are not in the best of taste, and Cassandra would perhaps have done well to destroy these instead of some of the material which did find its way into her wastepaper basket. The fact that she kept it may mean that the Halls of Sherborne were recognized – like Mr Waller? – as being totally unsympathetic characters to both sisters and that even in old age Cassandra did not see that it put Jane in a bad light to have these nasty little sentences left lying around.

Yet these are isolated offences. Jane's absorption with people and personality was usually indulged on a much milder level, generally finding its outlet in her novels. But it escaped sometimes beyond the boundaries of fiction and slipped out in wicked witticisms, for Cassandra's eyes alone, about acquaintances, never about real friends. Jane's novels show her powers of perception in a coolly circumspect way. Dashing off epistles to Cassandra she saw no need to be circumspect. Her writing then might have been in the nature of jottings in a diary, never intended to be kept for posterity's probings and psychoanalysis. Or it could be geared instead to Cassandra's interests, containing the kind of gossip she wanted to hear. References to the family, domestic affairs, travelling arrangements, clothes and so on take up a great deal of space, as they would in any correspondence between sisters. As a rule, world-shattering events do not, which is normal enough. And a little light-hearted wit at the expense of people whom one does not much like is, rightly or wrongly, quite normal, too.

Jane's enjoyment of this practice was well illustrated when she reported that a local acquaintance, Mrs Powlett, was 'at once expensively & nakedly dress'd; – we have had the satisfaction of estimating her Lace & her Muslin; & she said too little to afford us much other amusement'.[9] The timeless observation on this lady's clothes would be appreciated by any woman who has ever been astounded that a wispy bit of chiffon suspended on a pair of thin shoulder straps can sometimes cost more than the wardrobe housing it. Another acquaintance, Lady Sondes, made a surprise marriage, upon which Jane remarked: 'Provided she will now leave off having bad head-aches & being pathetic, I can allow her, I can *wish* her to be happy.'[10] Jane thought her ladyship 'an impudent Woman'[11] as well as an affected one and probably despised her on both counts. She had no time for the mannered posturings of the society in which she moved, even though as a girl she had conformed to convention enough to be mistakenly called affected herself. Invariably she had a forthright and unpretentious outlook and was not impressed by silly or impudent people. She saw through the veneer to the person beneath and could not resist ridiculing what she found.

Unluckily for any notion of getting a well-balanced picture of Jane from her letters, Cassandra later destroyed a number of them, wholly or in part – with the best protective motives, one hopes, but with disappointing consequences for us. Jane herself would probably never have believed that any of them would be on show for the world to read after she was gone, for she did not live long enough to realize how lasting her fame would be. But Cassandra did. And one cannot help having the occasional nagging doubt that Cassandra was at all times the eminently sensible sister she appears at first sight to have been, ever selfless, never misguided and with all her actions intelligently directed towards preserving Jane's image to the best advantage after her death. For most of the time, Cassandra was indeed Jane's *alter ego* – Jane certainly thought so – but, deep down, when older, it would be surprising if she never knew moments of irritation at still playing second fiddle to a long-gone younger sister who had always deferred to her in the past; and perhaps she allowed this to influence her a little.

Their niece Caroline protested years later at the publication of Jane's correspondence, and the reason she gave – that the public would not be interested – was the only one she would have felt it proper to offer, no doubt. But Caroline could well have wondered what imp of mischief guided her surviving aunt's hand when the tearing-up was in progress. The one valid excuse for Cassandra's odd exercise in selectivity would be her unworldliness, with publication never even occurring to her as a remote possibility. If this is so, she would have been most unhappy to know she had given Jane's future detractors such scope for their work.

Jane might also have been unhappy. A letter she wrote to Cassandra in 1804 contains the passage 'My Mother is at this moment reading a letter from my Aunt [Mrs Austen's sister-in-law Mrs Leigh Perrot]. Yours to Miss Irvine, of which she had had the perusal – (which by the bye, in your place I should not like) has thrown them into a quandary . . .'[12] The sentiment which she bracketed would probably strike a chord with most of us, though very few of us are condemned to be judged by our letters after we are dead.

However, Jane was not trying to be a candidate for canonization, so she could always have pointed out to the more unyielding of her critics that a little malicious humour adds spice to the dialogue of any novel and keen observation of faults and weaknesses provides the salt and pepper on the prose. And she would have taken pleasure in adding that too bland a dish might have been served up by an authoress fully entitled to join the angels.

*

Unaware of censure to come, Jane quietly went on corresponding with her sister and dutifully passing on all the news. Delicacy of expression certainly was a hallmark of her novels, but her letters do display a coarser sense of humour at times, more typical of the Regency period. From the Victorian era right up to the Second World War, the frankness of eighteenth-century speech was socially unacceptable; but none of Jane's little lapses from perfect taste would shock anyone now. There are two small instances in the novels, as Park Honan mentions in his biography of her. On her brother Frank's ship some sailors had been lashed for insolence, mutiny and sodomy, and the information had obviously been passed around the family. Thus, in *Mansfield Park*, the not-entirely-respectable Mary Crawford, an admiral's niece, refers to Rears and Vices and coyly says – just in case her sober audience has not picked it up – that no one must accuse her of making a pun.[13] A similar sortie into the realms of the *risqué* – cut from the second edition of *Sense and Sensibility* – is where Jane includes a passage which treated lightly the idea that Colonel Brandon might have an illegitimate daughter.[14] He was destined to marry one of the joint heroines, so the question of his chastity must be handled with care! Jane's editors did not want readers to know how broadminded her views on morality actually were.

But with Cassandra she felt she could be as broadminded as she liked. Describing an evening at the Assembly Rooms in Bath, she wrote that she had

> Mr Evelyn to talk to, & Miss Twisleton to look at; and I am proud to say that I have a very good eye at an Adultress, for tho' repeatedly assured that another in the same party was the *She*, I fixed upon the right one from the first . . . Mrs Badcock & two young Women were of the same party, except when Mrs Badcock thought herself obliged to leave them, to run round the room after her drunken Husband.[15]

The calm tolerance wavered a fraction in the same letter when she felt that Lord Craven's 'little flaw of having a Mistress now living with him at Ashdown Park, seems to be the only unpleasing circumstance about him'[16] but soon restored itself, when she saw 'nothing to be glad of, unless I make it a matter of Joy that Mrs Wylmot has another son & that Ld Lucan has taken a Mistress, both of which Events are of course joyful to the Actors . . .'[17]

When on a visit to a pupil at a smart and expensive boarding-school, she examined her surroundings and later pronounced judgement to Cassandra: 'The appearance of the room, so totally un-school-like, amused me very much . . . & if it had not been for some naked Cupids over the Mantlepeice, which must be a fine study for Girls, one should never have Smelt Instruction.'[18]

She was easy-going where her close friend Martha Lloyd was concerned, too. Quiet Martha, smallpox-scarred like her sister Mary, led a most correct social life, and the references Jane made to her harmless conquest of a married clergyman have a fun-loving pretence of disapproval in them. 'Martha & Dr Mant are as bad as ever,' she told Cassandra; 'he runs after her in the street to apologise for having spoken to a Gentleman while *she* was near him the day before. – Poor Mrs Mant can stand it no longer; she is retired to one of her married Daughters.'[19] And a week later:

> Martha pleases herself with beleiving that if *I* had kept her counsel, you wd never have heard of Dr M.'s late behaviour . . . I am willing to overlook a venial fault; & as Dr M. is a Clergymen their attachment, however immoral, has a decorous air.[20]

Jane was an outspoken advocate of birth control long before it ever officially existed: 'Mrs Tilson's remembrance gratifies me . . . but poor Woman! how can she be honestly breeding again?'[21] The only cure she could suggest, however, was self-control – a unilateral business unfortunately. 'Good Mrs Deedes! . . .' she sympathized, when another Kent friend embarked on a further pregnancy. 'I wd recommend to her & Mr D. the simple regimen of separate rooms.'[22] Her niece Anna, eldest child of James by his first wife, married a young clergyman, Ben Lefroy, and had four children in fairly quick succession. Jane's reaction belongs to our time, not hers: 'Poor Animal,' she wrote, her metaphor more feeling than flattering, 'she will be worn out before she is thirty. – I am very sorry for her. – Mrs Clement too is in that way again. I am quite tired of so many Children. – Mrs Benn has a 13th.'[23] However, Jane's pity for Anna was misplaced; far from being worn out at thirty she lived to be nearly eighty.

If Jane can justly be accused of having a coarse streak, she must be given credit for innate sensitivity in some respects at least. In her day epilepsy was not recognized as an illness but thought, in its most severe form, to be madness. And among all her gentle high-lighting of human frailty she never once put a mentally weak person into her novels nor made any reference to a village idiot – in an age when, perhaps owing to inbreeding, nearly every village had its quota. Her poor brother George may not have lived with the family, but his sister did not forget him.

Stark tragedy of any type never showed its face in her works, even though it touched the Austens on many occasions, as in such a large family it must. Her brothers Frank and Charles fought in the Napoleonic Wars, but she does not tempt fate by ever describing battles. And the execution of her cousin Eliza's husband could have provided the basis of a successful novel in less sensitive hands than Jane's, but she never mentions the French Revolution. One of her cousins, Jane Williams, was killed in a carriage accident, but the only overturning of a carriage in any of Jane's works occurs in *Sanditon*, almost before the book begins, and with nothing worse than a sprained ankle. On Jane's twenty-ninth birthday she lost a friend, Mrs Lefroy, wife of the Rector of Ashe near Steventon, killed in a fall from a horse. Yet people all ride their horses in her novels with perfect safety, no greater evil befalling them than in *Pride and Prejudice*, when Jane Bennet makes her equestrian arrival at Netherfield in a downpour and catches a streaming cold. Finally, no one at all dies 'on stage' in her works. More than one of Jane's brothers lost wives in childbirth, and Cassandra lost a fiancé from a contagious disease. Jane's delicacy prevents her from putting into her books such every-day occurrences as either of these events would then have been and thereby distressing the people closest to her heart.

If as a result of this deliberate restraint she is to be accused of being incomplete and insensible – Charlotte Brontë's impassioned declaration[24] – then so be it. Jane had her reasons, which have to be respected.

*

The snobbery that pervaded Georgian life had its effect on Jane and on her work; it was imbibed like mother's milk by her and everyone else as a kind of social religion. Her world was narrow, and it would have taken a great philosopher and a great rebel, as well as a great writer, to deny the precepts by which she was reared. Though there were a few free-thinking female eccentrics breaking out among artists and the nobility, rebel philosophers did not abound amid the middle-class ladies of rural Regency England. So all Jane's heroines marry reasonably well, in a material as in a spiritual sense. It would be strange if they did not. Any fiction of the time with romance as its mainspring required gentlemen like those Jane created, able to support brides in the style to which they hoped to become accustomed. Romantic fiction usually supplies this even now.

Money is undoubtedly on everyone's mind in Jane's books, as it is in many of today's best-selling novels. But the charge of undue concentration upon money is less likely to be levelled at modern works, dealing though they may with the unscrupulous acquisition of massive wealth by aggressive men and women, than it is at Jane's stories, with their elegant characters, whose inherited cash is never sullied by the tiniest whiff of skulduggery and whose good manners are never spoiled by the slightest show of temper.

The worst that Jane produces is constant discussion, usually among amusingly silly matrons, about how much capital – and resulting income – prospective spouses of either sex may be worth or how far individual charms might go towards enabling one to be traded for the other. Charlotte Heywood, in Jane's unfinished novel *Sanditon*, when suspected of aiming too high and setting her cap at a handsome baronet, says carefully: 'Sir Edward Denham, with such personal advantages may be almost sure of getting a woman of fortune, if he chooses it.'[25] And Jane, tongue in cheek, adds: 'This glorious sentiment seemed quite to remove suspicion.'[26] That in itself removes suspicion from her, of taking too seriously most of her characters' preoccupation with rich matches, even though to throw oneself away without a thought for finance was represented as disobliging the family, as poor Mrs Price did before the opening of *Mansfield Park*. David Cecil comments, regarding Jane's thesis, that it was wrong to marry for money but silly to marry without it.

As far as class snobbishness goes, Jane was not guilty of it in her personal life. 'Mr Deedes & Sir Brook – I do not care for Sir Brook's being a Baronet,' she declared, 'I will put Mr Deedes first because I like him a great deal the best . . .'[27] Sir Brook Bridges was the eldest brother of her own brother Edward's wife; and the Godmersham Park circle did seem at times to bring out Jane's small store of latent rebelliousness against the establishment, thankful though she was for its bounty through Edward. She was not as frequent a visitor to Godmersham as Cassandra, so perhaps did not feel so absolutely at home there. She certainly broke with all the traditions of snobbery by making a friend of the Knight family governess Anne Sharp, whom she would have encountered while staying at Godmersham. Corresponding with Anne, she wrote on a slightly more intellectual plane than when writing to the rather prosaic Cassandra. But the fact that she flouted the tacit rules by treating a governess on com-pletely equal terms might have helped to give rise to one of the Knight offspring, Edward's eldest daughter Fanny, referring somewhat scornfully to Jane. In a letter written when she was the middle-aged Lady Knatchbull – and might have been expected to look with mellow leniency on an aunt who she knew was devoted to her – she dismissed both Jane and Cassandra as lacking refine-ment and exhibiting what, from her lofty pedestal, she described as commonness. If, Fanny observed, it had not been for the kind guidance of the family's benefactress Mrs Knight – herself a Knatchbull by birth – her aunts would have spent their lives beyond the social pale. She ended this denunciation with a defiant flourish, cannily shifting responsibility for it to her 'pen's end', which had, she implied, quite carried her away.[28]

This was a sadder lapse of true refinement than ever Jane had sunk to, for Fanny had been her favourite niece, and they had enjoyed a close correspondence, mostly as a vehicle for Fanny to pour out her problems about countless beaux and be comforted, congratulated or advised by her understanding aunt. But the understanding would no doubt have been extended to other out-pourings. Jane, more than posterity, would have forgiven the quicksilver cruelty on the 'pen's end', which could not be halted and of which she herself had often been guilty. And she would have recognized that Fanny – who was, incidentally, writing at the time to a sister – probably felt quite secure in eternal privacy. History has a habit of repeating itself.

*

It is a pity that, out of all the Austen household, Jane is the only one of whom we have no properly authenticated portrait or outline, except what, in his *Facts and Problems*, Dr R.W. Chapman called 'a disappointing scratch'.[29] This part-coloured, part-sketched work by Cassandra is regarded as our only definitive guide to Jane's appear-ance. Yet, while the upper face is painted in, is the lower part of the picture really much more than a caricature? Cassandra could pro-duce very sensitive portraits, but she was a natural caricaturist too, as her original illustrations to Jane's youthful skit, *The History of England*, show. In that little *tour de force*, Mary Queen of Scots – Jane's 'bewitching Princess'[30] – who brought to a sticky end all the men who ever rallied to her cause, simpers prettily, a sugary Lorelei, while the over-painted, predatory profile of Elizabeth I – 'Murderess of her Cousin'[31] – would seem, if it had been executed a couple of centuries later, to owe a lot to Walt Disney's Cruella De Vil or Snow White's wicked stepmother.

It seems unbelievable that Cassandra would have seriously wanted to send her closest sibling into immortality with a shrewish, humourless mouth and arms pugnaciously folded as if she had just quarrelled with the artist. Yet the picture really does give the impression of being intentionally unflattering and turned out in a hurry, moreover, which casts doubts as to whether Jane properly sat for it. If everyone had been pleased with it, would not Cassandra have repaired the right eye, which is placed oddly in the face, to say the least? (Later artists have painted softer versions of this, re-siting the offending eye.) Why this should have been left around for posterity is a puzzle. Where is the great sweetness of manner and light-hearted wit always under the surface, waiting to bubble over, which we are told personified the real Jane? Nowhere to be seen here. However, the picture rests now in the National Portrait Gallery, a permanent monument to Cassandra's concept of her sister. Cassandra did once paint another view of Jane, out of doors and, most annoyingly, from the back. It tells us nothing about her.

There are two attractive silhouettes which are presumed to be of Jane, often reproduced. They face in opposite directions and were obviously executed – one reputedly by Jane herself – some years apart. The face seems to be the same one and very pleasing to look at. However, silhouettes are always tantalizingly incomplete, merely whetting the appetite.

A portrait which could perhaps represent her in the minds of many of her readers, and is in keeping with early descriptions of her, is the very youthful one which was, for a long time, attributed to Zoffany. More recently this has been thought to be by Ozias Humphry and, alas, depicting someone else with the same name –

Jane Motley Austen (later Mrs Campion), yet another of Jane's cousins.[32] However, there are serious flaws in the arguments supporting this theory.

Admittedly the girl in the portrait has straight hair, whereas Jane's was supposed to be fashionably curly – a fiction upheld successfully by many young women in the past, sharing bedrooms with sisters who were also remarkably blessed with natural curls! But many people with genuinely curly hair find variations in it from time to time, depending on weather, state of health, recent cutting and so on. Jane herself once indicated that, while her shorter strands of hair did not need the help of curl-papers, the heavier hair lurking under her cap was straight.[33] Her hair may well have been of this type, or why should she have needed to be 'curled out' by the deft Mr Hall when wanting to look her best for an evening in London?

It would be very satisfying to feel that this charming full-length adolescent figure, with a pleasing and cheerful face, is of the Jane we know. The picture was owned for nearly fifty years by Dr Thomas Harding Newman, Fellow of Magdalen College, Oxford, who received it in 1831 as a legacy from his stepmother. She had been given it by Colonel Thomas Motley Austen, cousin of Jane the author and brother of Jane Campion. If this were indeed a portrait of his sister (and not of the author, as the recipient and her stepson believed) it was an astonishing gift for the colonel to have bestowed on someone outside the family. Mrs Campion was only a few months younger than her famous cousin; she lived to be over eighty and was no doubt at the height of her powers when the portrait changed ownership. She would surely have wanted to keep a painting of herself and might have been expected to protest at such high-handedness on her brother's part. However, the loss of a dead cousin's picture, executed presumably on the one occasion she had stayed with her father's relatives in Kent when she was about twelve, would not, years later, be of such great importance to any of the Motley Austens who were still in possession of it.

The gift was ostensibly made because Mrs Harding Newman was an admirer of Jane's works, though there was possibly another more sentimental reason, investigated in Chapter 11 of this book. It was ultimately given away to a member of the Knight branch of the Austen family, John Morland Rice, whose brother's descendants inherited it; it is usually known as the Rice portrait

Jane died on 18 July 1817, at the age of forty-one, the first of all the Austen siblings to do so. Until recently it was thought that she had suffered from Addison's disease, but new theories have emerged that she might perhaps instead have had a different illness such as Hodgkin's disease; this can have periods of remission which would seem more in keeping with Jane's last months of life.[34]

A day or two after Jane died, Cassandra wrote to Fanny Knight, saying that she had lost such a sister and friend as could never be surpassed, adding, 'She was the sun of my life, the gilder of every pleasure, the soother of every sorrow.'[35] Of all the pictures of Jane that are left to us, the one that most closely suggests such a person is the Rice portrait – the idealist's view of her, maybe, but for ever young and happy.

PART II

The Men at Home

3

In Hampshire and Kent

IT can be no coincidence that the heroes of Jane's major works are two landed gentlemen, two clergymen and a naval officer. There are six completed novels, but *Sense and Sensibility* cannot really be deemed to have a male character who could be called a hero. However, even here Jane does not depart from her familiar pattern. Her two heroines join hands with yet another clergyman and a colonel – one of the armed services merely being exchanged for the other. She may have said that she was too proud of her gentlemen to admit that they were 'only Mr A or Colonel B',[1] but still she very sensibly depended for their occupations on the scene she knew, as she did with every other aspect of her writing.

Her father, the Reverend George Austen, was the doyen of the many clergymen in Jane's world. He was scholarly, kind and handsome, a good husband and father and a man who encouraged enterprise and individualism in his children, while at the same time doing his paternal best to secure them whatever influential benefits he could manage. It was an era when the first step on the ladder to promotion in any field was obtained by 'interest' – a mixture of nepotism and purchase – and it would have been abnormal for Mr Austen not to do everything he could for his sons in this way, as his own relatives had done for him in their turn. Dignified in personal bearing, he was equally dignified in his style of writing, and when he asked for favours he did not beg.

'I should not have introduced my son to your notice had I not been convinced that his merits as a man and a sailor will justify my recommendations,' he wrote, when seeking advancement for his son Frank.[2] His fatherly partiality was well under control, however, when he sent the fourteen-year-old Frank advice on how to be that man and sailor of merit.

> You may either by a contemptuous, unkind and selfish manner create disgust and dislike; or by affability, good humour and compliance, become the object of esteem and affection; which of these very opposite paths 'tis your interest to pursue I need not say.

This somewhat heavy style, redolent of the pulpit, was apparently transmitted along with the counsel, for it is similar to that which, in the fruitful days of his brilliant career, Frank himself adopted.

George Austen was as good-humoured himself as he desired his son to be – as opposed to being actually a humorist. His personality may have lost in sparkle what it had gained in intellect. Jane's love of reading was most likely inherited from him – he had five hundred volumes in his library – but her sense of fun came from her mother, who at her best could be as witty on paper as Jane herself. Though he could never have tried to emulate it, Mr Austen was the kind of man who would appreciate this facet of his wife's character without jealousy or disapproval.

He undoubtedly enjoyed his daughter's light-hearted writing. When he offered the publisher Cadell *First Impressions* (*Pride and Prejudice*) he was a little out of his depth; the publishing world was not his. However, he ventured into it on her behalf with his usual dignity, though clearly doubtful of success, since he inquired about the cost of publishing privately at the same time. This amount, if he were ever told it, must have proved too large to consider seriously. He had a great many sons to whom he owed responsibility and, like any man of his time, he automatically put their needs first. But his efforts for Jane and his gentle kindness made him a much-loved father, and when he died she praised his 'virtuous & happy life'[3] and spoke fondly of his tenderness and 'sweet, benevolent smile'.[4]

*

In such a close-knit group as the Austens were, all enjoying each other's company, laughing at the same jokes and visiting frequently, secure in the knowledge of affection returned, there could be no men in Jane's world who had such an enduring influence on her as her brothers. She made known her preferences and her displeasure from time to time, but whoever came briefly into her orbit outside the home – and there were a few whose impact was not as brief as all that – her brothers were the principal men in her life.

Of them all, the eldest, James, was the one who had the strongest early influence on Jane, but he lost it later; and though (or perhaps because) he was his mother's favourite, he is the only brother with whom Jane ever showed in her letters the slightest sign of continuing impatience. James was nearly eleven years older than she was, so he was rarely at home in her formative years, which made him the more noticeable to her when she did see him. He encouraged her reading, but, being the intellectual of the family, he favoured poetry himself – writing sonnets to two young women he admired – and scorned novels in general and female writers in particular. For the brother of an authoress, this was not exactly the most endearing of characteristics. He was an earnest, honest man, but had a rather lugubrious expression, with large mournful eyes set wide apart in a face that looked a little too narrow for its features. This soulful look gave the lie in some respects to his wit, much admired by the readers of a journal called *The Loiterer* which he produced while at Oxford. But on the whole his disposition tended to be moody and melancholy, unlike the rest of the Austens.

After some years as a Fellow of St John's, Oxford, which honour he had attained early, as Founder's Kin, James took holy orders. Before his father's retirement he was curate for him at Deane and Overton and stepped into the Steventon living in 1801. He had meanwhile made three proposals of marriage and taken two wives. First, in 1792, he married Anne Mathew of Laverstoke, daughter of a general and granddaughter of the Duke of Ancaster. An obviously delicate girl, she is immortalized in a picture of four ladies of the Mathew family, in which she stands behind her mother and sisters, brittle-framed, birdlike women, as similar as peas in a pod, and dwarfed by their hats, hairstyles and the gloomy severity of their stately sitting-room.[5] Anne died in 1795, leaving the two-year-old daughter, Anna, whom Jane so pitied later for her fecundity. It was soon afterwards that James made his romantic overtures to the just-widowed Eliza de Feuillide, helped out no doubt by the exciting atmosphere permeating the Steventon barn 'theatres'. But he was refused; Eliza had a dread of sinking into quiet obscurity as a parson's wife – a reaction mirrored by Jane in Mary Crawford's aversion to the idea of marrying a clergyman in *Mansfield Park*. Poor James, having set his sights on a stylish woman full of Continentally acquired grace, now, on the rebound, picked someone in total contrast: the plain, curt and uninspiring Mary Lloyd – younger sister of the more likeable Martha – whom he married in 1797. This rebuff must have caused a lasting coolness, for though Eliza became his brother's wife, by the time of her death in 1813 his little daughter Caroline, then nearly eight, had never once met her.[6]

Married to Mary, his mind and his actions do not seem to have been entirely his own. Welcomed warmly into the fold by Mrs Austen, she was soon revealed as a severe disappointment. She was possessive, not wanting James to visit his family; she took offence easily; she complained of poverty – despite, with £1,100 a year, being at this stage of her life better off than most of the other Austens; she expected to guide James's opinions (and did) and she was faintly hostile to her little stepdaughter Anna, causing James himself to lose interest for a while in the poor child. Jane tried in vain 'to give James pleasure by telling him of his Daughter's Taste, but if he felt, he did not express it'.[7] Worst of all for a man of his type, Mary was James's intellectual inferior.

He tried to combat this in an unbecoming manner, one which only aggravated Mary's hostility towards Anna: he would hold clever conversations with his daughter which were totally over his wife's head and would deride Mary tacitly in the process.[8] Needless to say, Anna's uncomfortable experiences turned her into a difficult child, Mary was disliked by her sisters-in-law, and James's temper shortened noticeably. This was a rather sad development all round. The whole family had liked Mary very much and Jane had been her close friend before her marriage. Mary was not an unkind woman at heart, but perhaps, finding it no easy matter to walk into a ready-made family – however small – and create a happy atmosphere, she reacted by becoming aggressive.

As early as 1798, the year after their marriage, Jane wrote to Cassandra at Godmersham:

James called on us just as we were going to Tea, & my Mother was
well enough to talk very chearfully to him, before she went to Bed
. . . James seems to have taken to his old Trick of coming to
Steventon, inspite of Mary's reproaches, for he was here before
Breakfast, & is now paying us a second visit.[9]

Several years later, when the women of the family were living
with Frank and his wife in Southampton, James had become something of a cipher in his own household, only asserting himself, it
would seem, in an irksome and ineffectual way again. 'I am sorry &
angry,' wrote Jane this time, 'that his Visits should not give one
more pleasure; the company of so good & so clever a Man ought to
be gratifying in itself; – but his Chat seems all forced, his Opinions
on many points too much copied from his Wife's, & his time here is
spent I think in walking about the House & banging the Doors, or
ringing the Bell for a glass of Water.'[10]

The scholarly James may have belonged to that inarticulate
band who, the more they realize they are at odds with others around
them to whom they should be close, the more they seem unable to
communicate. Elizabeth Jenkins says in her Austen biography that
'in his contacts with daily life his inner self was sometimes concealed
behind a mask of gaucheries and irritations, quite foreign to the
social graces of his family'.[11] Intelligent man that he was – even if
not keenly perceptive on a social plane – he must have been aware
of these shortcomings, and awareness could only worsen the
situation.

Yet despite a certain amount of isolation, James may have been
happier with the woman who so annoyed her in-laws than they
would have been ready to believe. He paid lip-service to wedded
bliss, at least, for on his fifteenth wedding anniversary he wrote
Mary a poem; its last lines ran:

Then read, my love, these artless lays
And blush not at a husband's praise,
Whom fifteen years of love have taught
To prize your merits as he ought.[12]

*

James and his Mary bestowed on Jane an inestimable if unintentional gift, their son James Edward – blond, good-looking and easy-going, whose companionship she enjoyed immensely – as well as their daughter Caroline, who, along with Anna, were quite clearly the nieces and nephew who valued Jane the most. All three tried their hands at writing. James Edward – who later took the name Austen-Leigh – met with some success and wrote an interesting memoir of his aunt as well. Caroline succeeded on a more modest scale with a collection of reminiscences about Jane and the rest of the family. But Anna, who like the others had passed everything she wrote to Jane for encouragement and criticism and whose cosy memories of her aunt were all of laughter, jokes and happiness, was so saddened when Jane died that she threw away her unfinished manuscript and abandoned the idea of ever writing a novel again. All three of James's children gave Jane great pleasure but James Edward particularly so.

When he was in his final year at Winchester, she displayed her understanding of the difficulties of youth, especially at a boys' boarding-school. 'Now,' she declared, 'you may own, how miserable you were there; now, it will gradually all come out – your Crimes & your Miseries . . . & how often you were on the point of hanging yourself . . .'[13]

He had just embarked at that time on a novel but lost two chapters of the manuscript. 'It is well that *I* have not been at Steventon lately, & therefore cannot be suspected of purloining them . . .' she told him. 'I do not think however that any theft of that sort would be really very useful to me. What should I do with your strong, manly, spirited Sketches, full of Variety & Glow?' And it was here that she recorded her most famous observation on her own work, continuing: 'How could I possibly join them on to the little bit (two Inches wide) of Ivory on which I work with so fine a Brush, as produces little effect after much labour?'[14] But Jane knew she did herself an injustice. She would not have exchanged those perfect miniatures she created on her two-inch bit of ivory for all the spirited sketches ever written. But it was typical of her to create confidence in James Edward by belittling her own work while encouraging his.

It was for James Edward (whom she just called Edward) that one final accolade was reserved. He was the favourite, and later heir, of her aunt Mrs Leigh Perrot, so he did not need any of Jane's money on her death. But he was the person to whom she wrote her last complete known letter, dated 27 May 1817 and sent from Winchester, where, accompanied by Cassandra and escorted on horseback in pouring rain by her brother Henry and her nephew William Knight, she had driven in his parents' carriage in order to stay near the doctor who made an eleventh-hour attempt to cure her. She began the letter cheerfully but could not maintain it in that vein; nor did she need to. She was not afraid to let him see how she faced death, with courage and humility: 'God bless you my dear Edward. If ever you are ill, may you be as tenderly nursed as I have been, may the same Blessed alleviations of anxious, simpathizing friends be Yours, & may you possess – as I dare say you will – the greatest blessing of all, in the consciousness of not being unworthy of their Love. – I could not feel this. – Your very affec: Aunt J.A.'[15]

*

Jane begins one of her best-loved novels with the words 'Emma Woodhouse, handsome, clever and rich, with a comfortable home and happy disposition, seemed to unite some of the best blessings of existence . . .' She could with very little alteration have applied these words to her brother Edward. He was a plain man rather than a handsome one, but he had a good brain and was undoubtedly rich – and with *his* comfortable home and happy disposition the blessings were there for him in full measure.

Edward was the brother for whom Jane perhaps felt the least spiritual affinity but the most actual gratitude. From 1809 up to the end of her life eight years later he provided the roof over her head, and his ability to do so was due to a mixture of good luck – in the fact that his father's benefactor, Thomas Knight of Godmersham, had no grandchildren – and good sense in making the most of his chances.

When it was clear that the estates of the Knight family were to have no heir, the Knights thought once more of their kinsmen the Austens, who were in the opposite situation, having a plethora of potential heirs but limited wherewithal. Thomas Knight the elder had looked after George Austen, and Thomas Knight the younger was prepared to do the same for one of his sons on a much grander scale. The eldest Austen boy, James, was ineligible, earmarked in everyone's minds to be the heir of not only his own father but, more importantly, Mrs Austen's brother – though in the event James was disappointed in the latter expectation. The next available boy was Edward, to whom the Knights offered a wonderful future, including the Grand Tour at the age of twenty-one, training in running the estates which were to be his hereafter and marriage to a beautiful, well-bred girl.

Edward was an even-tempered, amiable, practical man, sensible without being in any way intellectual. All these qualities made him very good with young children, which was fortunate, as he had eleven of them. Jane was witness to his kindness: 'I know no one more deserving of happiness without alloy,' she wrote.[16] And in return one of his sons became her youngest recorded male admirer. George, self-styled 'Itty Dordy', showed at the age of three exceptional devotion to his Aunt Jane, who, with her usual far-sighted realism, commented:

> My dear itty Dordy's remembrance of me is very pleasing to me; foolishly pleasing, because I know it will be over so soon. My attachment to him will be more durable; I shall think with tenderness & delight on his beautiful & smiling Countenance & interesting Manners, till a few years have turned him into an ungovernable, ungracious fellow.[17]

In 1791 Edward was the first of the Austen brothers to marry. His wife Elizabeth, third daughter of Sir Brook Bridges of Goodnestone, Kent, was a woman 'of great worth', to use Jane's words, and the marriage was a fruitful one. Jane had in Elizabeth a sister-in-law who was able to play the piano; they both liked country dances and sent each other new pieces of music to try out, having to copy it laboriously themselves. Elizabeth also had the means to entertain her husband's sisters lavishly at her first home Rowling, then later at Godmersham Park. Her many pregnancies failed to spoil her looks, and even Jane – not the most ardent visitor at 'lying-in' levees – was impressed after one new baby arrived to see that Elizabeth looked really pretty, clean and tidy, with a becoming cap and a spotlessly white and orderly dress. Elizabeth, lucky enough to be well attended, did not of course have to do anything but sit and be attired. But she nevertheless aroused comparisons with James's wife Mary, who was not neat enough in her appearance and did not bother about wearing a dressing-gown.

The sight of Mary apparently sufficed to put Jane off the idea of childbirth for life. Elizabeth was a better advertisement – until one day in 1808 when she was thirty-five and had just given birth to a healthy boy. It was her eleventh confinement in fifteen years – a strain on even the most cherished constitution – and it killed her.

At such a time, all the family would come to the rescue of the children. Jane had recently gone home after a visit to Godmersham, and Cassandra had taken her place, to arrive just in time for the birth with all its extra unexpected activity, grief and chaos. Jane's part in the drama was therefore on the sidelines but very useful; two of Edward's boys, Edward and George – Itty Dordy, by now thirteen, and his brother fourteen – came to stay to be looked after by Jane and their grandmother at Southampton. Jane bought their mourning clothes and kept them occupied with outdoor walks, river expeditions and a variety of indoor games – 'bilbocatch . . . spillikins, paper ships, riddles, conundrums, and cards'[18] – everything in fact that she could think of to take their minds off their loss. She dealt with death and its aftermath efficiently, but her sympathy for Edward was great and she was relieved to be able to write nine days later:

> All that you say of Edward is truly comfortable; I began to fear that when the bustle of the first week was over, his spirits might for a time be more depressed; and perhaps one must still expect something of the kind.[19]

Though Jane's fears were not realized, Edward did remain faithful to Elizabeth's memory, breaking with male Austen tradition. Each of Jane's other brothers lost his first wife and replaced her later; Edward alone did not and spent forty-four years a widower – longer than Jane's whole life. Until her own marriage Fanny acted as hostess for him, dominating him slightly as Elizabeth and her mother had. Despite this, Jane liked Elizabeth's mother Lady Bridges but was rather in awe of her, perhaps a feeling picked up from Edward or just an instinct (reinforced by atmosphere or even subtle hints?) that she was indeed thought unrefined. After all, if this had never been discussed by the Bridges-Knight-Knatchbull family, how did Fanny know it to repeat later?

After Fanny became the second wife of the middle-aged Sir Edward Knatchbull, her sisters took her place and kept Edward from loneliness in his Kent and Hampshire homes. Apart from a lawsuit over a rival claim to the Chawton properties, which gave him some temporary distress in 1816, he led a prosperous and peaceful existence.

Jane was not as close to Edward as Cassandra was. He and Cassandra had similarly down-to-earth minds – uncluttered with very much beyond practical matters perhaps – and they were completely at ease with one another. But he was a good host to both sisters; at Godmersham they lived very splendidly, and their normal length of visit, to make the long journey worth while, was a month or more.

The house is a grand Palladian mansion with a red brick front, wide wings, handsome pedimented windows and a door-case with Tuscan columns. Symmetrical and gracious, it is set off by a wooded hill behind and an open aspect to the fore. Edward, master of all he surveyed and much more besides, dined fashionably late at six o'clock and kept a very good table, groaning with excellent food and wine, as much appreciated by all the children who joined the adults for meals as by his visiting relatives and a steady stream of other guests. Occasionally Jane would contrive to be left to her writing while everyone was employed elsewhere. 'I am all alone,' she wrote once. 'Edward is gone into his Woods. – At this present time I have five Tables, Eight & twenty Chairs & two fires all to myself.'[20]

It was after his wife's death that Edward gave his mother and sisters their Chawton home. Chawton House had been let, but the lease had now expired and he decided to use it for himself and his family as an alternative home, so Jane had more opportunity of seeing all the Knights than she had had before. The boys were a little too occupied with exclusively physical pursuits – hunting and shooting, like their father and uncles – and too bored by aesthetic pleasures to satisfy their aunt completely.[21] But Fanny, bringing vicarious romance and amusement into Jane's life through her letters, was a perpetual joy to her. James had provided her most agreeably with Anna, James Edward and Caroline; but Edward's eldest daughter, she felt, surpassed them all. 'You are inimitable, irresistible,' she told Fanny. 'You are the delight of my Life.'[22] Anna and Fanny, both twenty-four in the year Jane died, were to remember her in such different ways that it is sad to know, with hindsight, of their usually astute aunt's unconcealed preference for the less appreciative niece.

For one who, like his mother, was marked out by the gods for a long life, it is amazing to read the constant references in Jane's letters to Edward's poor health; though perhaps it should not be quite so surprising considering that in this respect he was a true son of Mrs Austen, who had celebrated the Christmas of 1798 with over a month's nebulous illness requiring much dosing and bed-rest – a tiring business for everyone else. She had cocooned herself against nervous attacks in a manner worthy of Mrs Bennet, by demanding not to be told news of James's wife's accouchement in November (the birth of James Edward) until it was all over and eventually 'made her *entrée* into the dressing-room through crowds of admiring spectators', where the family all drank tea for the first time in five weeks.[23] Six months later Edward, not to be outdone, went on a trip to Bath for his health, accompanied by his wife and family, Mrs Austen and Jane. He was thirty-one at the time and embarking on half a century and more of stringent medical care.

Jane's letters throughout her remaining years are full of concerned observations about Edward – with everything in the world he could wish for except good health – or, in the case of her other brothers, Charles suffering from rheumatism and boils on his neck,[24] Henry with a pain in the face or a deranged stomach,[25] James's gums in a bad state[26] and Frank having a cough.[27] One by one she laments that they have 'a sad turn for being unwell',[28] but her own health does not seem to occupy her mind much until the days of her last illness. It is ironic to consider the amount of time she spent in worrying about or ministering to brothers who lived so much longer than she did – one of them into his nineties. And she spent quite a long time actually nursing her favourite, Henry, when in 1815 he had 'a fever – something bilious but cheifly Inflammatory'.[29] But that would have been a labour of love, for there was no one in the world whose society she would rather share than Henry, even when he was not at his customary glowing best.

4

'Not a Mind for Affliction'

HENRY was the one Austen brother whose intelligence and personality promised more than were ever fulfilled. Some of the failure was due to the fact that he had a mercurial temperament and two false starts in the three occupations he selected for himself, the first apparently uncongenial and the second unsuccessful. But also he was the one in the middle – with no rich relations to cushion the Austen poverty like his older brothers and no naval career watched over by acquaintances with Admiralty influence like the younger ones.

In the same way as his brother James, he went to Oxford when, in 1788, a vacant Fellowship as Founder's Kin arose; and this was the first of the troubled choices of his life, for he had wanted to accompany his cousin Eliza to France instead. Then in 1793 he enlisted in the Oxford militia, whereas his father had hoped he would follow him into the Church as James had done.

On the surface it would seem that the life of a militia captain, as he became, should have suited Henry. He was six feet tall, the handsomest of the brothers, a dazzling asset in any social gathering, a lively and entertaining conversationalist and possessed of a keen if unduly optimistic mind – the kind which may be more suited to making snap decisions and *bons mots* than to accumulating wealth or committing pearls of literature to paper. He was also, like all the Austen men, fond of outdoor sport, so would presumably have been a good shot, a good horseman and equally at ease on the field or in the officers' mess. This first career of his probably earned him his bride. Eliza de Feuillide, who had rejected the clergyman James, was more impressed by the dashing soldier in his red coat, ten years her junior, and married him in 1797. In many respects they were well matched despite the age gap, both being very sociable and sophisticated. Mrs Austen, however, was unhappy about it. In *Jane Austen's Literary Manuscripts* Brian Southam comments that Eliza's letters to Philadelphia Walter show her to be, like Jane's creation Lady Susan, 'witty, shrewd, calculating, flirtatious, jealous of her reputation, yet unable to preserve herself from scandal, a heartless mother, domineering with men, and glorying in their adoration, but essentially shallow in her feelings'. Her portrait, suggestive of a Greuze or Fragonard, with its luminous dark eyes larger than the rosebud mouth, thin tip-tilted nose and pointed chin, does indeed look appropriately like a self-satisfied little fawn – a type of woman unlikely to recommend herself to a mother-in-law. And Mrs Austen had known Eliza a long time. She was also worried about young Hastings de Feuillide, who suffered from epilepsy like her own son George. Poor Hastings was shortly to die, and Henry and Eliza never had children of their own; but Mrs Austen, not gifted with prescience, was wise to be afraid.

Meanwhile Henry, quite untroubled, launched himself into his wife's world and realized his earlier ambition; after the Peace of Amiens in 1802, they travelled to France to try to reclaim some of the de Feuillide estates. But they failed and were almost interned, having only Eliza's fluent French to thank for their escape back to England.

Eliza must have brought a touch of exotica into the lives of her sisters-in-law, though this would not have bowled Jane over as it had Henry. According to his beloved, the doting Henry was so in love with her that he could deny her nothing, and she had her own way every minute of the time. Eliza expected as much; she had written with the same hyperbole about her first spouse, never having learned that boasting detracted from her appeal – at least to other women. It says much for Jane's loyalty to Henry that she did not make this trait the butt of her wit. But Eliza was partially exempt from open derision; she was Mr Austen's niece. Jane must have suffered at times, but she suffered in silence.

After the first year or two, Henry (or Eliza) decided that he should give up his military career. He became a partner in a firm of London and Alton bankers, living fashionably in Upper Berkeley Street, on the corner of Portman Square, and enjoying the social round which they both loved.

When *Sense and Sensibility* was accepted by the publisher Thomas Egerton and sent to the printers in 1811, Jane went to London to read the proofs and stayed with Henry and Eliza. Henry collected Jane at the house of a cousin, where for a quarter of an hour he put 'Life & Wit into the party',[1] then whisked her off to his home, by now moved to Sloane Street, among green fields through which they could walk into the centre of London to go shopping. Immediately Jane was caught up in Henry and Eliza's lively whirl, and because it was Henry's she derived more pleasure from it than she might otherwise have done – for on the whole she did not like the city life of London any more than that of Bath.

One evening Henry and Eliza held a musical party for sixty-six people. Professional musicians performed and everything was laid on most elegantly. Though Jane's party-going days were by then over, she enjoyed the company of the other guests, particularly, one supposes, Mr Wyndham Knatchbull, who described her as a pleasing-looking young woman. She was happy enough with this compliment, coming as it did about ten years after a Regency lady could have expected to be called young; but while she could not resist telling Cassandra about it, she dismissed it in the same breath: 'that must do; – one cannot pretend to anything better now.'[2]

The party had been a success from the host's and hostess's point of view, too. Cassandra received a report of it all:

> There were many solicitudes, alarms & vexations beforehand of course, but at last everything was quite right . . . Mr Egerton & Mr Walter came at ½ past 5, & the festivities began . . . At ½ past 7 arrived the Musicians in two Hackney coaches, & by 8 the lordly Company began to appear . . . The Drawg room being soon hotter than we liked, we placed ourselves in the connecting Passage, which was comparatively cool, & gave us all the advantage of the Music at a pleasant distance, as well as that of the first veiw of every new comer. – I was quite surrounded by acquaintance, especially Gentlemen; & what with Mr Hampson, Mr Seymour, Mr W. Knatchbull, Mr Guillemarde, Mr Cure, a Capt Simpson, brother to *the* Capt Simpson, besides Mr Walter & Mr Egerton . . . I had quite as much upon my hands as I could do . . . The Music was extremely good . . . & all the Performers gave great satisfaction by doing what they were paid for, & giving themselves no airs. – No Amateur could be persuaded to do anything. – The House was not clear till after 12. – If you wish to hear more of it, you must put your questions, but I seem rather to have exhausted than spared the subject. – This said Capt. Simpson told us, on the authority of some other Captn just arrived from Halifax, that Charles was bringing the Cleopatra home, & that she was probably by this time in the Channel – but as Capt. S. was certainly in liquor, we must not quite depend on it.[3]

Jane never lost an opportunity to glean information about her seafaring brothers whenever she was among people who might know shipping movements; but it sounds a slightly too Bacchanalian gathering for accurate information to be passed around.

The description of the party is evocative – doubly so. Cool air blows along that draughty passage between the two assembly rooms at Highbury's Crown Inn. Or, Mary Bennet – the easily persuaded amateur – has mercifully been prevented this time from doing anything in front of a bored Netherfield audience. And Jane for a moment becomes Emma Woodhouse or Elizabeth Bennet, young and beautiful, instead of Jane Austen, thirty-five and now a fraction past her best.

Eliza naturally knew plenty of French *émigrés*, so they visited Henry's home too. Jane espoused the general British Francophobia at that time and, while getting along famously with the elderly Comte d'Entraigues, a 'very fine-looking man with quiet manners . . .' she unblushingly added, 'If he wd but speak english, I would take to him.'[4]

Henry's life did not continue in this style for very much longer. Eliza suffered a slow decline in health, and in April 1813 she died. At first Henry was struck down by his loss but proved resilient like all the Austens and recovered well. Jane went to stay with him in Sloane Street a month later to soften the blow a little.

Her journey there was, as it turned out, not at all in the nature of a mission of mercy to a soul in torment. On the contrary, Henry brought a carriage to Chawton to fetch her, and they seem to have had a delightful trip back to London in a burst of unseasonably early summer weather. They took the Guildford-Esher-Kingston route rather than their usual Bagshot road, and both of them thought it much better, Jane noting that it was the same mileage. It was particularly pretty, she said, from Guildford to Ripley, and she had never seen the country from the Hog's Back to such advantage. They dined at Esher – if only she had said where! – 'upon veal cutlets & cold ham, all very good'.[5]

A significant passage now occurs in this letter to Cassandra for anyone interested in the possible model for Highbury in *Emma*. If there *is* a recognizable place on which Jane based her village, it has often been presumed to be Leatherhead, because of its proximity to Box Hill and the fact that it contains a Randalls Park and a Knightley in the church records. But Esher has – or had – the right ambience, too, an equally accurate geographical location, a Weston Green just down the road and the Bear Hotel, an attractive model for the Highbury Crown. It remains only for Mr Knightley's Donwell Abbey to be nestling beneath 'a Mr Spicer's Grounds at Esher which we walked into before our dinner' and from which

> the veiws were beautiful. I cannot say what we did *not* see, but I should think there could not be a Wood or a Meadow or a Palace or a remarkable spot in England that was not spread out before us, on one side or the other . . . Upon the whole it was an excellent Journey & very thoroughly enjoyed by me; – the weather was delightful . . . Henry found it too warm & talked of its' being close sometimes, but to my capacity it was perfection.[6]

Drifting beside Jane and Henry around the grounds of a large house with lovely views, in sunshine almost too warm for comfort, one could fancy oneself on the strawberry-picking expedition to Donwell, with 'its ample gardens stretching down to meadows washed by a stream . . . and its abundance of timber in rows and avenues . . .'[7] Donwell was admittedly in the valley beneath 'a bank of considerable abruptness and grandeur, well clothed with wood'[8] and watered by the handsome curve of the river, but we have only to transpose positions, with Jane and Henry looking down on it from the top of the bank, and we are there. It was not many months after this that Jane began writing *Emma*. If Leatherhead can be thought to be her Highbury, the supporters of Esher's claims may surely have a valid point, too.

Jane always said that her locations, as well as her characters, were those of her own imagination. But there are exceptions to every rule, and in one case she must definitely have had a real town in mind and given it a pseudonym. In Chapter XLII of *Pride and Prejudice* Elizabeth Bennet asks the chambermaid in the inn at Lambton if Mr Darcy is in residence at his home Pemberley, the local great house, and receives 'a most welcome negative'. The following morning she and her aunt and uncle repair to the house to look at it, only to discover to Elizabeth's horror Mr Darcy himself in the grounds. She apologizes in embarrassed haste, which seems to have transmitted itself right through to Jane, for she makes Elizabeth say to him: 'Before we left Bakewell, we understood that you were not immediately expected . . .' There is no possible way, from the manner in which the story has progressed, for the party to have inquired at Bakewell as well as Lambton; Bakewell has not been mentioned up to that point. Therefore they must be one and the same town.

To return to the question of Esher, *Emma* being a light and glowing novel, one feels that its location could well have been determined on just such a sunny journey as the one Jane made that May with Henry.

*

After some weeks Henry was a great deal better, Jane wrote to their brother Frank, and he was able now to see Eliza's death as a release. 'His Mind is not a Mind for affliction,' she observed, for once stating the blatantly obvious. 'He is too Busy, too active, too sanguine.'[9] Indeed, this sanguine nature – 'perpetual sunshine' Anna described it – could be a trial under conditions when others around him felt far from sanguine, such as when his bank failed three years later and he became bankrupt, dragging down, to a lesser degree, a few other members of the family with him. However, for the moment, optimism stood him in good stead.

'Sincerely as he was attached to poor Eliza moreover,' Jane went on in her letter to Frank, '& excellently as he behaved to her, he was always so used to be away from her at times, that her Loss is not felt as that of many a beloved Wife might be . . .'[10] Emma Woodhouse might well have spoken in this way of Mr Weston, in the unlikely event of the more robust Mrs Weston's early demise. 'Rather an easy cheerful-tempered man, than a man of strong feelings; he takes things as he finds them, and makes enjoyment of them somehow or other,'[11] Mr Weston would be sad for a while, but he is such an outgoing character that he would find it impossible not to recover briskly and completely. Henry Austen is often thought to be very much like the witty and tolerant Henry Tilney of *Northanger Abbey*, and Tilney certainly seems to have borrowed these qualities from his real-life namesake. But we see quick glimpses of Henry in others as well – not just *Emma's* Mr Weston but his son Frank, charming but thoughtless enough to let secrets slip out to the distress of someone he loves, which Henry was shortly to do to Jane. And there have been suggestions, too, that the even less scrupulous but equally charming Henry Crawford of *Mansfield Park* bears in some respects a slight likeness to Jane's dearest brother – which she may never have consciously intended, even though, like Henry Tilney, he has had Jane's most cherished male name bestowed upon him.

The following spring, 1814, she stayed with Henry again – this time in a flat he had moved into over his office at 10 Henrietta Street, Covent Garden – and there he read the manuscript of *Mansfield Park*. He admired Henry Crawford 'as a clever, pleasant Man' (seeing the similarity perhaps!) and made interested comments about the manuscript in general.[12] Henry was always Jane's most enthusiastic supporter and the most helpful to her in all aspects of her writing.

Helpfulness and enthusiasm can get out of hand, however. Jane had always wanted her work to be anonymous. But Henry, on a trip to Scotland, heard the new, anonymous, novel *Pride and Prejudice* being praised by two titled women and could not resist divulging that the author was his sister. Jane was quite seriously upset, not, surely, because some people who meant nothing to her had been told she was a writer but because of the breach of confidence. However, it was Henry who committed that breach, so complete forgiveness was a foregone conclusion.

But, overall, Henry's pride in her, his help with reading her novels and his way of dealing with publishers was invaluable – and he carried it off with panache. In 1803 *Northanger Abbey* – under its original title *Susan* – had been sold to a dilatory publisher, Crosby, who held on to it for thirteen years without doing anything further with it. Henry bought it back for what Crosby had paid, then, on leaving, told him casually that it was by the author of the famous *Pride and Prejudice*. He also paid Jane the compliment of sending a copy of *Pride and Prejudice* to his late wife's godfather, the former Governor-General of India, Warren Hastings, who praised it warmly.

During the period in 1815 when *Emma* was in the hands of the publisher Murray (whom Jane summed up as 'a Rogue of course, but a civil one',[13] since he had been very complimentary but only offered her £450 for it, wanting the copyrights to both *Mansfield*

Park and *Sense and Sensibility* into the bargain), Jane was with Henry once more. He had moved, yet again, back to the Sloane Street area, in Hans Place. And it was here that he was taken ill, with Jane on hand as willing nurse. Henry stayed in bed, living on 'Medicine, Tea & Barley water',[14] while Jane remained near at hand in the same room, writing – and there were not many people with whom she would have relaxed enough to do that. He was not so ill that he could not pen a letter of gentle complaint to Murray, but soon after that he had a relapse. Jane sent for Cassandra, James and Edward, who all arrived to stay to help him back into the world or see him with all possible comfort out of it. This trauma lasted a week, after which Henry recovered steadily and everyone except Jane went back to their own quarters. Fanny Knight came along later to help Jane preside over Henry's convalescence.

Henry had been attended by a young and efficient apothecary named Mr Haden, who diagnosed 'general Inflammation'[15] – a safely conservative judgement to make. He justified his presence by taking twenty fluid ounces of blood from the patient – who behaved well throughout his indisposition, being 'ready to swallow anything'.[16] Once Henry was back on his feet, if a little unsteadily, Mr Haden became a friend who joined their small circle socially and was attentive in a non-medical way to both Jane and Fanny, though it must be admitted that the self-confident young niece seems to have made more headway with him than the aunt. One evening they held a small party, at which Mr Haden arrived first for dinner, then,

> from 7 to 8 the Harp; – at 8 Mrs L. & Miss E. [Latouche and East] arrived – & for the rest of the Eveng the Drawg-room was thus arranged, on the Sopha-side the two Ladies Henry & myself making the best of it, on the opposite side Fanny & Mr Haden in

two chairs (I *beleive* at least they had *two* chairs) talking together uninterruptedly.[17]

She suspected Mr Haden was stretching out Henry's illness as an excuse to keep seeing Fanny: 'still they will not let him be well.'[18]

However, Mr Haden took some trouble over Jane, too; he knew the Prince Regent's Carlton House librarian, the Reverend James Stanier Clarke. As the prince was an admirer of Jane's novels, having a set in each of his homes, Clarke was able to provide an interesting tour of the Carlton House library for her, at 'Prinny's' personal invitation. None of this, incidentally, made her like the prince himself, because of his callous treatment of his wife Caroline of Brunswick – who was, three years after Jane's death, destined to endure the extreme humiliation of being locked out of Westminster Abbey at her husband's coronation. The future George IV was negligent enough as a spouse already, provoking Jane into remarking:

> Poor Woman, I shall support her as long as I can, because she *is* a Woman, & because I hate her Husband – but I can hardly forgive her for calling herself 'attached & affectionate' to a Man whom she must detest . . .[19]

The prince's new and immensely grand library, classical, colonnaded, multi-coloured marble on the outside and inner entrance and richly hung with Gothic furnishings, fan-vaulting and stained glass within, was so bizarre that it quite bedazzled her, and when she got home she was not sure whether she had actually been asked to dedicate *Emma* to His Royal Highness or not. Somewhat to her dismay it was confirmed that the prince would like it; she complied, upon which Clarke delicately suggested that she might like to dedicate her next book to the prince's new son-in-law, who later became King of the Belgians and Victoria's 'dearest Uncle Leopold'. However, since his suggestion embraced the subject matter too – a 'Historical Romance illustrative of the History of the august house of Cobourg'[20] – Jane declined firmly, knowing she must keep to her own style. 'And though I may never succeed again in that, I am convinced that I should totally fail in any other,' she answered.[21]

One way and another, both directly and indirectly, Henry had a great influence on Jane's social pleasures and literary acclaim, as well as making the execution of her work happier by his avid reading of her stories and appreciation of her humour. In addition he attended to all the troublesome administrative and business matters concerned with publication. To crown it all, for this period of her working life, when her early efforts finally bore fruit and she had begun to come into her own, he was always at hand to advise, with no wife or family to distract his attention from her. There were women friends in the background – one in Hanwell whom he wanted to introduce to Jane, one at Sunninghill, causing a detour on a long drive so that Jane could meet her, and others. But he did not marry his second wife Eleanor Jackson until after Jane had died, so for four important years he was more or less hers to command. During this period he had at last done what his father had wanted, though not for the reasons George Austen would have chosen. Bankruptcy turned him to the Church, and he was ordained in 1816, becoming Curate of Chawton for a short time. His sermons were spirited and rather evangelical in style – not for Henry the ponderous, sleepy delivery – but perhaps because of his lack of traditionalism, and his late start, he did not climb really high in the Church. Immediately following Jane's death in 1817 he worked for a while in Berlin as Chaplain to the Embassy, then, when James died two years later, he held the Steventon living. Following that, he was for many years Perpetual Curate of Bentley, near Alton. He retired to France but came back home – almost – to die in Tunbridge Wells at the age of seventy-eight. His niece Anna said he remained young-looking to the end.

Jane's devotion to him had been such that she could not bear the thought of a certain irritating Mr Wigram, a Godmersham guest, bearing his illustrious Christian name. 'They say his name is Henry,' she told Cassandra. 'A proof how unequally the gifts of Fortune are bestowed.'[22] And when she died there were three beneficiaries in her will. The principal one was her sister, to whom she left all her possessions and money, except for two other legacies: two sums of fifty pounds each – about a fifth of her net assets – to Henry and to his French housekeeper, a Madame Bigeon, whose cooking and company she had enjoyed on those happy visits to London.

5

The Admirals

HAVING endowed them with one intriguing chameleon among their collection of sons, Mother Nature returned to basics three years later and blessed Mr and Mrs Austen with Frank. Dry and plain-spoken, he was a reliable and stalwart if unimaginative person, never put off any course of action he wanted to take, even as a curly-headed toddler. And, like a more celebrated but less lucky admiral, Horatio Nelson, he apparently never knew the meaning of fear.

When Frank was twelve he went to the naval academy at Portsmouth, becoming a midshipman at fourteen and an officer at eighteen. At twenty-one he sailed in his sloop the *Lark* in the squadron of ships escorting Caroline of Brunswick to England for that miserable marriage of hers, at twenty-three he blockaded Cadiz in his ship of the line, the *London*, and two years later, already a commander, he took dispatches in his sloop the *Peterel* to Nelson at Palermo to warn him of the French fleet's escape from Brest.

Thus by the age of twenty-five he was moving upwards at a very brisk rate – owing partly to the Napoleonic Wars being conducive to quick promotion, and partly to friends in high places. While none of this could have been accomplished if he had not been courageous, clear-thinking and hard-working, nevertheless he had to thank one or two influential people for help along the way. The Austens knew Warren Hastings, not only through Mr Austen's niece Eliza but also because Hastings's little son had for most of his very short life been brought up in England by them during the early days of their marriage. In 1794 Mr Austen wrote to thank Hastings for his friendly help on Frank's behalf; so they had cast their bread on the waters to good effect. In addition to this valuable connection, they also knew Admiral Lord Gambier, and it was he who in 1798 put in a word for Frank with Lord Spencer, the First Lord of the Admiralty. Not unnaturally, promotion followed. 'Frank is made –' Jane wrote delightedly on 28 December. 'He was yesterday raised to the Rank of Commander . . .'[1] So, knowing from first-hand how the system worked, Jane was able to apply it when promoting her heroine's brother William Price in *Mansfield Park*.

Frank went from strength to strength, attacking French ships off Marseilles and taking a prize, *La Ligurienne*, of 42-guns. Then, as a result of this success, he joined the 98-gun *Neptune* as Flag Captain. After blockading Napoleon's Boulogne flotilla, he was transferred to the *Canopus*, with 80 guns, a former French Admiral's ship captured at the Battle of the Nile. Nelson, hearing of this, commented in a letter to Lord Moira that Frank could not be better placed. 'Capt. Austen I knew a little of before,' he added. 'He is an excellent young man.'[2] The excellent young man followed Nelson to the West Indies in pursuit of French ships in 1805 – nearly seven thousand miles there and back – only a few months before Trafalgar. But when the battle which ended Nelson's life was joined, Frank missed it, having been ordered to Gibraltar to collect provisions.

Distressed at Nelson's death, he wrote to his fiancée Mary Gibson, a Ramsgate girl, with his accustomed pedantry:

I never heard of his equal, nor do I expect again to see such a man. He possessed in a superior degree the happy talent of making every class of persons pleased with their situation and eager to exert themselves in forwarding the public service.[3]

His opinion of the enemy commander Admiral Villeneuve, whom he met later, was lukewarm; he struck Frank as having 'not much the appearance of a gentleman'.[4] Jane was clearly not the only Austen to have a low opinion of those unfortunates who did not speak English!

Frank was still captain of the *Canopus* – and had just fought in the victory at St Domingo, where all the French ships were destroyed or taken – when he married Mary. He had been engaged to her for three years. Jane liked her and had written to Cassandra earlier: 'He is in a great hurry to be married, & I have encouraged him in it . . .'[5] But Frank soon had to go off to sea again. The missives he sent Mary must have been more like war communiqués than great love-letters, if the one about Nelson was a fair example, but he at least paid her the compliment of talking to her on equal terms. Mary Gibson was not remarkable for her intelligence, but probably Frank did not want the cut and thrust of lively discussion, being quite content with making statements and receiving placid acknowledgements.

This was the period when they lived with Mrs Austen, Cassandra, Jane and Martha Lloyd at Southampton – a house full of women, where, when Frank was not at sea, he occupied himself with quiet homely pursuits in keeping with theirs. Once, forced to stay indoors with a hacking cough, he spent his time making fringe for the drawing-room curtains.[6] He seems to have been dextrous in all kinds of ways. When he was home on leave over ten years earlier, he had made and turned a delicately beautiful little ivory pounce box, gold inlaid. Jane wrote to Cassandra then that 'He enjoys himself here very much, for he has just learnt to turn, and is so delighted with the employment, that he is at it all day long.'[7]

Someone once said to Frank that he must have been the model for *Persuasion*'s Captain Wentworth, who had also acquitted himself with credit at St Domingo. However, he very sensibly disclaimed this, for Jane would not have been likely to base the debonair Wentworth on him, except to borrow from his professional background, of which she needed some inside knowledge in order to achieve accuracy. But Frank did admit that he thought parts of the character of Wentworth's homelier friend Captain Harville were drawn from him. 'At least,' he added, carefully qualifying such a rash statement, 'the description of his domestic habits, tastes and occupations have a considerable resemblance to mine.'[8] Harville 'drew, he varnished, he carpentered, he glued; he made toys for the children, he fashioned new netting-needles and pins with improvements; and if everything else was done, sat down to his large fishing-net at one corner of the room'.[9] In short, he liked to keep busy and could turn his hand to anything, and so could Frank. There is also a little similarity between Frank and the blunt, equable Admiral Croft in the same novel. Both Harville and Croft are slightly older men – an image which does not seem wrong for Frank, even when he was young. This is strange, since the images projected by Henry and picked up by Jane in her portrayals are mostly youthful ones, though Henry was Frank's senior.

Perhaps it was this prematurely elderly streak in Frank that made him so utterly dependable – and on one occasion preferable to her Henry in Jane's eyes. When Henry committed the foul crime of telling the Scottish ladies that Jane had written *Pride and Prejudice*, she wrote to Frank on his ship the *Elephant*, then sailing in the Baltic:

A Thing once set going in that way – one knows how it spreads! – and he, dear Creature, has set it going so much more than once. I know it is all done from affection & partiality – but at the same time, let me here again express to you & Mary my sense of the *superior* kindness which you have shewn on the occasion, in doing what I wished.[10]

Frank's cautious dependability may have helped to ensure his longevity. Sickness and war shortened the life expectancy of sailors – at a time when, by modern standards, *all* life expectancy was short enough – yet Frank lasted the longest of all Jane's brothers, surviving to be ninety-one. While luck must have played its part – at that time a ship sunk in the middle of the ocean would almost inevitably take the whole crew with it – nevertheless it is difficult to visualize Frank, in combat, behaving with the recklessness that brought about Nelson's end or taking any course of action in peace or war that would unnecessarily risk the lives of his men or himself. At Trafalgar, Nelson had tempted fate by going on deck wearing the four stars of his orders like glittering targets on his jacket and refusing to change, while Vice-Admiral Lord Collingwood adopted customary procedure and went out to meet fate halfway, by donning silk stockings and easily removed shoes in case of emergency amputation. Frank quite definitely belonged to the school of Collingwood.

Jane was extremely proud of Frank and followed his career with keen interest. When he had captured *La Ligurienne* against very heavy odds in 1800, he had written home a typically modest letter, upon which she fondly remarked: 'We have at last heard from Frank . . . of his Promotion he knows nothing, & of Prizes he is guiltless.'[11] And earlier still, at the outset of his career in 1791, when in her little *History of England* she mentioned Sir Francis

Drake, she added 'I cannot help foreseeing that he will be equalled in this or the next Century by one who tho' now but young, already promises to answer all the ardent & sanguine expectations of his Relations & Freinds.'[12]

Years later, in 1813, when she was staying at Godmersham, she noticed that there was yet another *Life of Nelson* in print, by Southey this time. 'I am tired of Lives of Nelson,' she said,

> being that I never read any. I will read this however, if Frank is mentioned in it. – Here am I in Kent, with one Brother in the same County [Charles, at The Nore] & another Brother's Wife [Frank's Mary, at Deal], & see nothing of them – which seems unnatural – It will not last so for ever I trust. – I shd like to have Mrs F.A. & her Children here for a week – but not a syllable of that nature is ever breathed.[13]

A guest at Godmersham herself, she was not in a position to invite them but was clearly champing at the bit because Edward had not yet done so.

Mansfield Park contains not only naval references but scenes at Portsmouth. For this Jane needed a touch of authenticity and asked Frank if she might mention his ship the *Elephant* '& two or three other of your old Ships? – I *have* done it, but it shall not stay, to make you angry.'[14] It did not make Frank angry, for not only is the *Elephant* there but the *Canopus*, too. And for good measure she included two ships of Charles's, the *Endymion* and the *Cleopatra* – so that he should not feel left out, perhaps. Having so exemplary an elder brother must at times have made Charles wish he had joined the Army instead.

The only hiccup it would seem that Frank suffered in his success story occurred two years after Trafalgar, when he was

Captain of the *St Albans* and was in command of a flotilla for the East India Company's trading in China – which included the transport of opium. His name was mentioned then in connection with the possible murder of a local Chinese. However, after six weeks' delay, he was cleared without too much fuss and continued his discreet opium run home again, quietly depositing his cargo at Deal. He brought with him thirteen ships worth two million pounds and received a thousand guineas from the company as a reward. From 1811 he served in the North Sea and Baltic for three years, after which he spent a welcome period on shore and did not set out on his travels again until after Jane had died.

Probably the most calm and cool of all the Austen sons, Frank was only rivalled in his physical stoicism by Charles. In fact, not surprisingly, the admirals were the only two of Jane's brothers who did not seem to suffer like their mother from those wearisome nerves.

Calmness is sometimes the result of inner peace, and Frank was a very religious man, always kneeling in church in defiance of the contemporary fashion for remaining standing and quite unconcerned about being different from his fellow officers – even to the extent of never swearing. He was different in a few other ways, too, rather oddly. It is one thing to be coolly coherent in the face of danger and never to show panic. But it is quite another to be able to call out with measured serenity to an officer swimming in the sea close by, 'Mr Pakenham, you are in danger of a shark. A shark of the blue species.'[15] And a man who could dismiss a five-year-old chronometer as unreliable because in that time it had lost five minutes must have been a difficult person to live with, one would think.

Yet Frank married two women who seemed to manage it cheerfully. Mary Gibson probably had an easy-going temperament in any case. Jane liked her and befriended her from the outset, encouraging Frank to marry her – not that he would have been daunted in the face of anyone's coolness. The friendship lasted; when she had other diversions to occupy her in the comfort of Godmersham, Jane had wanted to be able to have Mary to share them on a visit with the children – most of whom were too young to afford Jane any keen interest in their own right.

Mary and Frank had six sons and five daughters, exactly matching Edward Knight's family, though they did not all survive. And, like Edward's wife, Mary died at the birth of the eleventh in 1823. Later, in 1826, Frank did something which would have delighted Jane; he married Martha Lloyd. Martha of course had lodged in his home twenty years earlier in crowded conditions and had had ample opportunity to discover if he were difficult to live with or not. She enjoyed belated prestige as his wife; he was made a Knight of the Bath in 1837 and Vice-Admiral in 1838. But she died five years later and never saw him reach, in 1863, the highest rank that the Navy has to offer, as Admiral of the Fleet Sir Francis Austen – at the ripe old age of eighty-nine.

*

Frank may not have been Jane's model for Captain Wentworth, but Charles definitely had a few characteristics in common with William Price of *Mansfield Park* – the same naval career and the same open temperament, full of happy energy. Charles was the only sibling whom Jane could call her little brother; the last in the family, he was over three years younger than she was. Charles had a sunny disposition – very nearly as buoyant as Henry's – and handsome features, adding up to great personal charm. When as a young man he departed from the old traditions and became the first Austen male to adopt the new short and unpowdered style of haircut, Jane's friend Mrs Lefroy was so taken with his appearance that she thought it made him even handsomer than Henry – a compliment indeed. But Jane was afraid that such an innocently *outré* experiment would incur brother Edward's disapproval and asked Cassandra not to tell him about it; Edward had not been well, and she feared 'it might fall on his spirits and retard his recovery'[16] – astonishingly expressing a similar level of concern to that which she later showed when the mother of all his children had just died.

Charles was an entertaining writer who sent highly readable letters home from overseas, then returned to the family bearing armfuls of presents. These dispensed, he would dine heartily, then go off and enjoy himself with boundless stamina at whichever local ball happened to coincide with his homecoming. It did not even have to be local, in fact, for he would happily ride thirty miles for the pleasure of dancing with pretty girls. But the irregularities of naval life meant that he rarely arrived to schedule – causing Jane many a minor anxiety:

> Charles is not come yet, but he must come this morning . . . The Ball at Kempshott [Lord and Lady Dorchester's mansion] is this Evening, & I have got him an invitation, though I have not been so considerate as to get him a *Partner*.[17]

He appears to have missed that particular event but contrived to get to another one a good deal later, arriving home 'on a Gosport Hack', immediately walking from Steventon to dine out at Deane, a mile or two away down the soggy, rutted November lanes, then 'danced the whole Evening, & to day is no more tired than a gentleman ought to be . . . It was a pleasant Evening, Charles found it remarkably so . . .'[18]

It was on another visit home, when Jane had just moved to Bath, that Charles presented two attractive topaz crosses on gold chains, one to Cassandra and one to Jane.[19] He had collected thirty pounds as his share of some prize money and, as usual, spent much of it on other people. 'Of what avail is it to take prizes if he lays out the produce in presents to his Sisters . . .' was Jane's rhetorical question. 'I shall write again by this post to thank & reproach him. – We shall be unbearably fine.'[20]

This gift achieved immortality when Jane put it into *Mansfield Park* as 'a very pretty amber cross . . . from Sicily'[21] which William Price gives his sister Fanny – who is genuinely horrified at being unbearably fine but nevertheless just as delighted as Jane with her cross. But fiction is made more complicated than fact, naturally. William Price, unlike Charles, cannot afford a chain to go with it, so that is supplied later – in circumstances causing even more distressed agitation to the inhibited Fanny – by her earnest but blinkered hero Edmund Bertram.[22]

Charles had begun his career by following Frank to the Royal Naval Academy at Portsmouth and becoming a midshipman on the *Daedalus* and the *Unicorn*. He saw action on the latter in 1796 and was commissioned at the end of the following year, aged eighteen. But from then on he was overshadowed by his brother. He fretted about this a great deal – fearing his career was at a stand-still – which was once more reflected in William Price's words, 'I begin to think I shall never be a lieutenant, Fanny. Everybody gets made but me',[23] to which Fanny begs him not to be so despondent: 'My uncle', she assures him, 'will do everything in his power to get you made.'[24]

Charles's worries were similarly echoed by Jane. 'I am sorry that our dear Charles begins to feel the Dignity of Ill-usage,' she was writing as early as 1798, when he was longing to get on to a frigate, with its greater chance of prize money. Then, with touching confidence, she added: 'My father will write to Admiral Gambier.'[25] And indeed Mr Austen did write, but Admiral Cambier had given up being obliging for the moment and replied that Charles should stay where he was, on the brig *Scorpion* until 'a proper opportunity offers & it is judged that he has taken his Turn in a small Ship . . .'[26] Rubbing salt in the wound, the admiral went on to say that Frank's next promotion was on its way. Jane felt for Charles, sinking, as she put it, into nothing but 'an humble attendant on the Hero of the peice . . . By what the Admiral says it appears as if he had been designedly kept in the Scorpion – .'[27]

In the end, despite all the initial nail-biting, it took Charles exactly the same length of time to become a commander as it had Frank, and in October 1804, at twenty-five, he was in charge of the *Indian* – only, however, an eighteen-gun sloop. He picked it up in the Far East but was then moved to the North American station, where he had to stay for six years.

This was a very long exile, and it prevented Charles from participating in battles which, though fraught with danger, could end up being profitable by way of prize money. Frank had at the time of Trafalgar written to his Mary bemoaning his missed chances through being at Gibraltar. How much more disappointed must Charles have been, confined to an area where there was no extra cash or glory but merely the dreary repetition of scouting the seas for deserters or illegal traders.

Charles was a conscientious and humane commander. He was distressed when he had captured a small French ship which then managed to wriggle free and escape. But, as he told Cassandra, resulting from this the real misfortune of the episode was a further loss, 'the lives of twelve of my people, two of them mids'.[28]

When he finally returned home in 1811, it was on the *Cleopatra*

– a frigate at last. When Jane had been discussing his possible home-coming at Henry and Eliza's musical party, her eagerness was under-standable. It was the first time he was to see England for nearly seven years. He brought a wife with him, Fanny Palmer, a daughter of the Attorney-General of Bermuda, and two small daughters, Cassy, who had suffered from seasickness, and Harriet, who seemed more seriously unwell. A third, Frances, was on the way, having no doubt guaranteed her poor mother a thoroughly dreadful Atlantic crossing, ordeal as it was under even the best conditions.

Jane was delighted to see Charles again, and like everyone else she approved of Fanny Austen, who was a fresh, pleasant-looking, pink-and-white blonde with a happy disposition to match that of Charles. But, to judge from her silhouette, she did not share Charles's elegant features and form – having a premature double chin and a pouter-pigeon figure.[29] Cassy took after her in appear-ance, though regrettably not in tranquillity.

'Poor little Love –' wrote Jane, 'I wish she were not so very Palmery . . . I never knew a Wife's family-features have such undue influence.'[30] And her criticism of Cassy did not stop there; she was the only really spoilt Austen child. Charles and his Fanny, lazily indulgent, were both unwilling to inject discipline into their family life. 'Charles's little girls were with us about a month,' Jane told Frank in the summer of 1813,

> & had so endeared themselves that we were quite sorry to have them go. We have the pleasure however of hearing that they are thought very much improved at home – Harriet in health, Cassy in manners. – The latter *ought* to be a very nice Child – Nature has done enough for her – but Method has been wanting; . . . She will really be a very pleasing Child, if they will only exert themselves a little. – Harriet is a truely sweet-tempered little Darling.[31]

Once back with her parents, Cassy's tantrums soon returned. Three months later Jane was writing from a large family house-party at Godmersham to Cassandra at Chawton: 'I should be very happy in the idea of seeing little Cassy again too, did I not fear she wd disappoint me by some immediate disagreableness.'[32] But she looked forward with unqualified pleasure to seeing her brother, whom she could rely on to be 'as happy as he can with a cross Child or some such care pressing on him . . . here they are safe & well, just like their own nice selves, . . . & dear Charles all affectionate, placid, quiet, chearful good humour.'[33] Jane smiled through gritted teeth and persevered with Cassy for Charles's sake, on one occasion sending her a little 'Happy New Year' letter, each word written backwards, and signed (with the old alternative of I for J) 'Ruoy Etanoitceffa Tnua, Enai Netsua'.[34]

At the Godmersham gathering Edward took Charles out shooting in a high wind, difficult though it made their sport. Charles, being used to icy winds and rough weather at sea, seems to have revelled in it, like Edward. 'This Cold weather comes very fortunately for Edward's nerves with such a House full,' said Jane, 'it suits him exactly, he is all alive & chearful. Poor James, on the contrary, must be running his Toes into the fire.'[35]

While James evokes a picture of *Emma's* John Knightley, never going out in bad weather – or any weather – if he could contrive to stay in his own home by his own fire, Edward and Charles conjure up the Musgrove and Hayter gentlemen in *Persuasion* – both of whom were called Charles – out in all weather enjoying blood sports and the open air.

During the period when he made this visit to Godmersham, Charles was stationed at The Nore. It was there in the following year, 1814, that his wife had a fourth daughter on board his ship. Both mother and baby died. Poor Fanny was only twenty-four and had never had much material benefit from being married to Charles – nor much comfort in her shipboard existence. He was left now with three little daughters, one of them, Harriet, diagnosed by an eminent London consultant, Sir Everard Home, as having water on the brain. In the midst of all his grief, Charles was sent to the Mediterranean.

While he was there an incident occurred – as in Frank's career – which placed his progress in jeopardy for a little while and strained his natural optimism even more. His ship, the *Phoenix*, sank in 1816 in a hurricane off Asia Minor, and he was court-martialled. However, from this point onwards his luck showed signs of changing. The blame was placed with the Greek pilots, and he was cleared. And soon afterwards he found his next wife.

He did not have to look very far, for he had known his bride-to-be for some time already. She was Harriet Palmer, Fanny's sister. A few years later he would have been prohibited by law from marrying his sister-in-law, but at that time there was no legislation against it, in the same way as there is none today. So Charles happily embarked on the prospect of producing another little brood with Palmery features.

The same year as the court-martial he paid a visit to Chawton with his children and their Aunt Harriet. The feeling of flurry comes through in Jane's letter to Cassandra, the housekeeper-in-chief, who was away at Cheltenham:

A Letter arrived for you from Charles last Thursday . . . & he writes principally to ask when it will be convenient to us to receive Miss P. – the little girls & himself. – They wd be ready to set off in ten days from the time of his writing, to pay their visits in Hampshire & Berkshire – & he would prefer coming to Chawton *first*. I have answered him & said, that we hoped it might suit them to wait till the *last* week in Sept:r, as we could not ask them sooner, either on your account, or the want of room . . . He does not include a Maid in the list to be accomodated, but if they bring one, as I suppose they will, we shall have no bed in the house even then for Charles himself – let alone Henry –. But what can we do? – We shall have the Gt House quite at our command . . .[36]

Chawton Great House probably came in very useful then. Charles appears, from other inferences here and there, to have been impulsive in his social decisions, like many nice, cheerful, charming people. Jane's letters frequently suggest that he either failed to turn up when expected, planned his timing awry and made a late entry (with family in tow at least once) in the middle of meals or announced his imminent arrival at awkward moments. He had grown used to the family making allowances for him from earliest times, no doubt.

But in any event, he was still Jane's lovable young brother, warm and encouraging like Henry, telling her how much he and his fellow officers enjoyed her novels, and he was always her 'dear Charles'. In return she had a special place in his affections; he kept a letter she sent him shortly before her death and wrote on the back of it, 'My last letter from dearest Jane'.[37]

In 1820 Charles married Harriet, and had four children by her, of whom two sons grew to manhood. Happily, his little daughter Harriet did not have water on the brain but survived, along with her two sisters, to a reasonable age. The youngest girl, Frances, married her cousin, Frank's son Francis, which might have ensured that the Austen features, in one line at any rate, predominated over the Palmer ones; however, they had no children. Though he was always short of money Charles did at least receive honours and promotion, as a Commander of the Bath in 1840 and Rear-Admiral in 1846, and still went on seeing action all over the world. In 1852, at the age of seventy-three, he was taking a steam sloop up the Irrawady in Burma when he contracted cholera and died – 'a great grief', one of his friends mourned, 'to the whole fleet'.[38]

*

Mary Lascelles, in *Jane Austen and Her Art*, says that Jane's naval officers never appear to have been taking an active part in the wars but 'enter very composedly as though returned from walking up partridges in the stubble'[39] and that it was rather disappointing not to have her heroes in general display 'a more personal type of fire'.[40] Indeed Admiral Croft and the three captains of *Persuasion* – Wentworth, Harville and Benwick – do seem very peaceable (one of them admittedly too much so), but surely that is part of being a gentleman. More fire is on show in Jane's seafaring characters when they are lower down the social ladder – the more lowly, the more fiery, in fact. In *Mansfield Park* William Price, the unsophisticated young midshipman struggling to reach lieutenant's rank, is allowed to crackle and glow rather more than the *Persuasion* captains; and Fanny Price's rough father, whose loud voice is bearable only when he is out in the open air and whose short, blunt sentences are laced with expletives toned down to suit the reader's sensibilities, produces one of the best hearthfuls of homely flames that Jane ever offers us.

She brings in her naval references as well as she can, but neither Frank nor Charles were the sort of brothers who would have recounted highly dramatic stories of their experiences for fear of frightening their womenfolk. In any case, they were obviously not braggarts and probably not great raconteurs; real men of action rarely are.

In her woman's world with all its cramped conditions and the restricted vision imposed upon it, Jane was in the same position as Fanny Price, sitting and listening to the men's talk of ships going in and out of Portsmouth harbour, or as Anne Elliot, who could only consult Navy lists for information. When helping her niece Anna with her novel-writing Jane advised her to

> Let the Portmans go to Ireland, but as you know nothing of the Manners there, you had better not go with them. You will be in danger of giving false representations. Stick to Bath & the Foresters. There you will be quite at home.[41]

If Jane had tried to take her fictional naval officers out of the drawing-room, she would have been entering the field of false representations. Like any other Regency woman, she was safer sticking to Bath and employing what Sir Walter Scott called 'the exquisite touch, which renders ordinary commonplace things and characters interesting'.[42]

Yet it is an intriguing thought to dwell on what occupation Jane might have followed if she had not been a woman but a Regency man. Edward's luck was unique, so she could not have emulated him. But with a choice of following James and Henry into the Church or Frank and Charles in the Navy, there seems very little doubt as to where Jane's inclinations would have taken her.

PART III

Cameos

6

Gentlemen Observed

MANY of the most engaging of Jane's fictional characters are the minor ones; they linger in the memory in some cases long after the main protagonists in the battle of the sexes have been forgotten. In just the same way, there are a variety of real-life characters of whom we are given a Jane's-eye view. They move about in her letters, clearly outlined, with flesh and blood and personality, never content to be the stationary Greek-tragedy mutes that stay obscurely in the background of the average family letter.

She passed briefly over mere physical characteristics, such as those of Benjamin Portal, 'whose eyes are as handsome as ever',[1] and lingered only a fraction longer on 'Sweet Mr Ogle. I dare say he sees all the Panoramas for nothing, has free-admittance every-where; he is so delightful!'[2] But she spent more writing-time on Henry's London apothecary-extraordinary Mr Haden, 'our Precious' as she called him.[3] She shared Fanny's enthusiasm for this gentleman, despite the fact that he had an unreasonable passion for music which she thought rather too intense. Other qualities compensated for this peculiarity, however: 'Then came the dinner & Mr Haden who brought good Manners & clever conversation.'[4] That was on 26 November 1815. A few days later, on 2 December, once again

Mr Haden was secured for dinner – I need not say that our Eveng was agreable. – But you seem to be under a mistake as to Mr H. – You call him an Apothecary; he is no Apothecary, he has never been an Apothecary . . . he is a Haden . . . something between a Man & an Angel . . .[5]

She was very nearly as taken with a political gentleman whom she met in Kent – very nearly, but not quite. Mr Stephen Rumbold Lushington of Norton Court, the Member of Parliament for Canterbury, flashed his politician's smile which charmed Jane but did not deceive her:

Mr Lushington goes tomorrow. – Now I must speak of *him* – & I like him very much. I am sure he is clever & a Man of Taste. He got a vol. of Milton last night & spoke of it with Warmth. – He is quite an M.P. – very smiling, with an exceedingly good address, & readiness of Language. – I am rather in love with him. – I dare say he is ambitious & Insincere. – He puts me in mind of Mr Dundas – . He has a wide smiling mouth & very good teeth, & something the same complexion & nose.[6]

The description falls short only in that we are not privileged to know what Mr Dundas looked like; but he was evidently handsome in a complacently conceited way – and florid, perhaps?

Jane's descriptions are often constructed so that Cassandra may laugh at her, since she realized that the best jokes are always those told against oneself. She had been to a dance, for Twelfth Night most likely, in 1799, where there were

more Dancers than the Room could conveniently hold, which is enough to constitute a good Ball at any time. – I do not think I was very much in request – . [She had, on her own admission, a cold that day with, it seems, a touch of conjunctivitis, so her lack of success was not really surprising.] People were rather apt not to ask me till they could not help it; – One's Consequence you know varies so much at times without any particular reason – . There was one Gentleman, an officer of the Cheshire, a very good looking young Man, who I was told wanted very much to be introduced to me; – but as he did not want it quite enough to take much trouble in effecting it, We never could bring it about.[7]

Just prior to that, at a Christmas gathering, she had written to Cassandra, 'Our Ball was very thin . . .' Perhaps the cold she caught in the New Year was already forging its punitive path through the neighbourhood. But Mr Calland, the Rector of Bentworth, seemed to prove that gentlemen who did not go to dances in order to dance were more highly prized, once they coyly allowed themselves to be chivvied into it, than those more amenable creatures who started out by doing what everyone had gone there for. Mr Calland, a soul palpably ready to be converted,

appeared as usual with his hat in his hand, & stood every now & then behind Catherine & me to be talked to & abused for not dancing. – We teized him however into it at last; – I was very glad to see him again after so long a separation, & he was altogether rather the Genius & Flirt of the Evening. – He enquired after You.[8]

Mr Holder, the tenant of Ashe Park, comes into a different category. She did not like the idea of her father's bailiff, John Bond, being taken on by him at the end of 1800, when the Austens were to move from Steventon, for she felt that he would not be such a good employer as Harry Digweed at Steventon Manor, who would have been willing to give John a post.[9]

She had been a regular visitor with her family and friends to Mr Holder's house, on one occasion being invited at the last minute, to make up numbers, no doubt, and

dine tete a tete with Mr Holder, Mr Gauntlett & James Digweed; but our tete a tete was cruelly reduced by the non-attendance of the two latter – . We had a very quiet evening, I beleive Mary [James's wife] found it dull, but I thought it very pleasant. To sit in idleness over a good fire in a well-proportioned room is a luxurious sensation. – Sometimes we talked & sometimes we were quite silent; I said two or three amusing things, & Mr Holder made a few infamous puns.[10]

One day shortly before they left for Bath she found herself in

a situation of the utmost cruelty. I arrived at Ashe Park before the Party from Deane, and was shut up in the drawing-room with Mr Holder alone for ten minutes . . . nothing could prevail on me to move two steps from the door, on the lock of which I kept one hand constantly fixed.[11]

Whether Mr Holder really did have a reputation for womanizing, or whether Jane was merely being whimsical about the preservation of her own good reputation, is hard to tell. But he was evidently not a favourite of hers or she would never have expressed her preference for John Bond going to work for Harry Digweed.

The other Digweed gentleman, the Reverend James, indulged

in his own piece of whimsy, which Jane passed on to Cassandra –
then in Kent – as she frequently did when men paid her sister
compliments

> James Digweed left Hampshire today. I think he must be in love
> with you, from his anxiety to have you go to the Faversham Balls,
> & likewise from his supposing, that the two Elms fell from their
> greif at your absence. – Was not it a galant idea?[12]

Jane's ability to dismiss gauche, silly or repulsive men was as
crisp in her early twenties as in her late thirties. In 1799 'Mr Gould
. . . walked home with me after Tea; – he is a very Young Man, just
entered of Oxford, wears Spectacles, & has heard that Evelina was
written by Dr Johnson'.[13] At Bath in 1801 she shrugged off Admiral
Stanhope as 'a gentlemanlike Man, but then his legs are too short,
& his tail too long'.[14] In 1808

> I have got a Husband for each of the Miss Maitlands; – Coln
> Powlett [recently deserted by his flighty wife] & his Brother have
> taken Argyle's inner House, & the consequence is so natural that
> I have no ingenuity in planning it. If the Brother shd luckily be a
> little sillier than the Colonel, what a treasure for Eliza.[15]

Since the Colonel in time became a Major-General, it is to be
hoped for England's sake that he was not as silly as Jane implied. In
1813 they had a visitor at Godmersham whom she did not like at
all: 'Mr Rob. Mascall breakfasted here; he eats a great deal of But-
ter.'[16] Three days later she had more to say of him: 'He talks too
much & is conceited – besides having a vulgarly shaped mouth.'[17]

The dismissal is gentler in her earliest days; but then the man
was most likely nicer and more deserving of her gentleness. With a

man who needed help she could be really kind, even if she could not resist describing the situation lightly. A Mr Fitzhugh, 'poor Man! is so totally deaf, that they say he cd not hear a Cannon, were it fired close to him; having no cannon at hand to make the experiment, I took it for granted, & talked to him a little with my fingers . . .'[18]

She watched with interest the chequered career of one Steventon neighbour, a son of the family of Deane House. He was a Royal Marine and had recently taken a bride with a murky past. 'Earle Harwood has been to Deane . . .' she wrote, '& his family then told him that they would receive his wife, if she continued to behave well for another Year . . . Earle & his wife live in the most private manner imaginable at Portsmouth, without keeping a servant of any kind.'[19] Eight months later she came to the conclusion that 'Earle's vanity has tempted him to invent the account of her former way of Life, that his triumph in securing her might be greater; – I dare say she was nothing but an innocent Country Girl in fact.'[20]

A few more months passed, and the romantic idyll nearly came to a premature end.

> Earle Harwood has been again giving uneasiness to his family, & Talk to the Neighbourhood; – in the present instance however he is only unfortunate & not in fault. – About ten days ago, in cocking a pistol in the guard-room at Marcou [St Marcouf, an island off the Normandy coast], he accidentally shot himself through the Thigh. Two young Scotch Surgeons in the Island were polite enough to propose taking off the Thigh at once, but to that he would not consent; & accordingly in his wounded state was put on board a Cutter & conveyed to Haslar Hospital at Gosport; where the bullet was extracted, & where he now is I hope in a fair way of doing well.[21]

One can only hope along with Jane that this proved the case and that poor Earle spent a happy life with his unacceptable spouse.

*

Marriage and romance figured as always in her letters, giving rise to studies of people and situations. For instance: 'Mary Oxenden, instead of dieing, is going to marry Wm Hammond.'[22] She usually went into more detail, of course, such as when the formalities of the dining table presented matchmaking problems. Jane reported:

> I could see nothing very promising between Mr P. & Miss P.T. [Mr Papillon and Miss Patience Terry]. – She placed herself on one side of him at first, but Miss Benn obliged her to move up higher; – & she had an empty plate, & even asked him to give her some Mutton without being attended to for some time. – There might be Design in this, to be sure, on his side; – he might think an empty Stomach the most favourable for Love.[23]

But another dinner fostered romance in rather an unpropitious atmosphere. The violent wind that felled the Steventon elms in November 1800 also wrought havoc at Ashe Rectory.

> where we sat down 14 to dinner in the study, the dining room being not habitable from the Storm's having blown down it's chimney . . . Rice & Lucy made love, Mat: Robinson fell asleep, James & Mrs Augusta [Bramston] alternately read Dr Jenner's pamphlet on the cow pox [and presumably vaccination] & I bestowed my company by turns on all.'[24]

A few months later, Jane announced blandly, 'Mr Rice & Lucy are to be married, one on the 9th & the other on the 10th of July.[25]

In the event, it was on the twentieth that the Reverend Henry Rice married Miss Lucy Lefroy.

Her cynicism about motives for and results of marriage was always just under the skin, ready to erupt. In one instance,

> Miss Sawbridge is married . . . Mr Maxwell *was* Tutor to the young Gregorys – consequently they must be one of the happiest Couple[s] in the World, & either of them worthy of Envy – for *she* must be excessively in love, & *he* mounts from nothing, to a comfortable Home.[26]

And in others: 'Dr Gardiner was married yesterday to Mrs Percy & her three daughters';[27] 'Miss Jackson is married to young Mr Gunthorpe, & is to be very unhappy. He swears, drinks, is cross, jealous, selfish & Brutal; – the match makes *her* family miserable, & has occasioned *his* being disinherited';[28] 'Mrs John Lyford is so much pleased with the state of widowhood as to be going to put in for being a widow again; – she is to marry . . . a man of very good fortune, but considerably older than herself';[29] 'The papers announce the Marriage of the Rev: Edward Bather, Rector of some place in Shropshire to a Miss Emma Halifax – a Wretch! – he does not deserve an Emma Halifax's maid Betty';[30] and 'Dr Phillot to Lady Frances St Lawrence. *She* wanted to have a husband I suppose, once in her life, and *he* a Lady Frances.'[31] The comments are all sour, and if one did not know that Jane would never have married out of the desperation which some of her acquaintances exhibited, she could well be thought jealous instead of just mildly scornful. Closer to home, one marriage which was about to take place, that of Anna to Ben Lefroy, disturbed her: 'We are anxious to have it go on well . . . he hates company & she is very fond of it; – This, with some queerness of Temper on his side & much unsteadiness on hers, is untoward.'[32] Genuine worry was uppermost here and genuine interest with a desire to help when advice was sought, as it often was.

Fanny Knight liked a Mr Plumtre of Fredville, Kent, who promptly obliged her by falling in love with her. Perversely, Fanny then developed doubts. She wrote to Jane, who assured her, 'I have no scruple in saying that you cannot be in Love.'[33] Fanny felt that Mr Plumtre was too quiet and retiring. Jane back-pedalled at that, pleading, 'is it not a fine Character, of which Modesty is the only defect?'[34] Fanny decided he was too good for her. Jane replied, 'As to their being any objection from his *Goodness* . . . I cannot admit *that*.'[35] Fanny also complained that he was not as sparkling as her brothers. Jane countered:

> There *are* such beings in the World perhaps, one in a Thousand, as the Creature You & I should think perfection, where Grace & Spirit are united to Worth, where the Manners are equal to the Heart & Understanding, but such a person may not come in your way, or if he does, he may not be the eldest son of a Man of Fortune, the Brother of your particular friend, & belonging to your own County . . . Wisdom is better than Wit.[36]

Then the true, cautious Jane came to the fore. Having tried to be just to Mr Plumtre, she fell back on her own maxim: 'I . . . entreat you not to commit yourself farther, & not to think of accepting him unless you really do like him. Anything is to be preferred or endured rather than marrying without Affection . . .'[37] Some time later Mr Plumtre paid court elsewhere, at which Fanny took a dog-in-the-manger attitude. Jane showed her first signs of losing patience: 'You did not chuse to have him yourself; why not allow him to take comfort where he can?'[38]

Five months before Jane's death Fanny became embroiled in a largely imaginary love affair with Mr Wildman of Chilham Castle, Kent, who later disappointed her. Jane obligingly provided consolation. 'My dearest Fanny, I cannot bear You should be unhappy about him. Think of . . . want of Money [a telling point!], of a coarse Mother, of Brothers & Sisters like Horses, of Sheets sewn across &c.'[39] Needless to say, when Fanny did marry, she took care to avoid all likelihood of such hardships. But Jane had spent as much effort on Fanny's requirements in the field of romance as she spent on all her brothers' requirements in the field of medical care.

She did not always view people's attachments with alarm, however, and was often delighted with what she considered a good match. For example, she hoped 'it is true that Edward Taylor is to marry his cousin Charlotte. Those beautiful dark Eyes will then adorn another Generation at least in all their purity.'[40]

But in a lot of marriages she did see food for thought – horror or pity. The case of Edward's sister-in-law, Harriot Bridges, created intermittent concern; her husband George Moore was the son of an Archbishop of Canterbury, but this did not endear him to Jane, who at first 'saw nothing in him to admire'.[41] Once, before a late-night supper, he had 'ordered his wife away, & we adjourned to the Dressing room to eat our Tart & Jelly . . . nothing seemed to go right with him.'[42]

During another mealtime at Godmersham she watched the suspect George closely, to see how he behaved to his wife on this occasion. 'Had I had no reason for observing what he said & did,' Jane told Cassandra, 'I shd scarcely have thought about him. – His manners to her want Tenderness – & he was a little violent at last about the impossibility of her going to Eastwell. – I cannot see any unhappiness in her however . . .'[43] 'I really hope,' she added later,

'Harriot is altogether very happy – but she cannot feel quite so much at ease with her Husband, as the Wives she has been used to.'[44]

Jane met the couple again at Godmersham five years later and studied them closely, as before.

> Oweing to a difference of Clocks, the Coachman did not bring the Carriage so soon as he ought by half an hour; – anything like a breach of punctuality was a great offence – & Mr Moore was very angry – which I was rather glad of – I wanted to see him angry – & though he spoke to his Servant in a very loud voice & with a good deal of heat I was happy to perceive that he did not scold Harriot at all. Indeed there is nothing to object to in his manners to her, & I do beleive that he makes her – or she makes herself – very happy.[45]

In just such a way does Emma Woodhouse's sister Isabella make herself happy with John Knightley, whose 'temper was not his great perfection',[46] and, in a less subtle manner, Charlotte Palmer of *Sense and Sensibility*, with her 'droll' husband whose every excess of rudeness merely draws from her more peals of laughter and wifely admiration.[47] Jane observed some strange partnerships in her social round, and mused on them to good effect.

*

Character cameos, in more novels than one could list, have been created very successfully from servants, yet this is one category of people of whom, in her works, Jane hardly seemed aware. She never gave them more than a line or two to speak; but this was not because they failed to exist for her but because she wrote only on subjects she knew about. Without indulging in intentional eavesdropping she had no way of knowing how servants talked or behaved in private – only how they behaved in front of their employers, which was usually very dull stuff, since the rule there was for silent self-effacement. So Jane, playing as ever for safety and knowing her limits, excluded servants unless they were absolutely necessary to the story or dialogue. And the males of her novels are indeed 'gentlemen' in particular and not men in general.

She did, however, mention servants in her letters sometimes. When the Austens were about to set up home in Bath she tried to cheer herself up with facetious remarks about the future household arrangements: 'We plan having a steady Cook, & a young giddy Housemaid, with a sedate, middle aged Man, who is to undertake the double office of Husband to the former & sweetheart to the latter.'[48] In the event a servant, James, whom they seemed to have discovered at Lyme, proved a treasure to them all.

> James is the delight of our lives; . . . My Mother's shoes were never so well blacked before, & our plate never looked so clean. – He waits extremely well, is attentive, handy, quick, & quiet, and in short has a great many more than all the cardinal virtues . . .[49]

But none of his virtues would have qualified him for status as a leading player on Jane's stage. Once below stairs, he would have been a mystery man. And mysteries were not Jane's speciality.

1 Jane's father, the Reverend George Austen
(1731–1805)

Private collection

2 Jane's mother, Mrs George Austen, née Cassandra Leigh
(1739–1827)

Private collection

3 Jane's sister, Cassandra Austen
(1773–1845)

By permission of the Jane Austen Memorial Trust

4

4 Jane's eldest brother, the Reverend James Austen
(1765–1819)

5 Jane's third brother, Edward (Austen) Knight
(1767–1852)

6

6 Jane's fourth brother, the Reverend Henry Austen
(1771–1850)

Private collection

7

7 Jane's fifth brother, Admiral of the Fleet
Sir Francis (Frank) Austen (1774–1865); portrait painted in 1806

8

8 Jane's younger brother, Rear-Admiral Charles Austen (1774–1865);
portrait painted in 1809

Private collection

9

10

9 Martha Lloyd (1798–1874),
later Lady Austen, who lived
with the Austen women for the last
decade of Jane's life and who
was her close friend

Private collection

10 Jane's nephew,
the Reverend James
Edward Austen-Leigh
(1798–1874)

Private collection

11

11 Steventon Rectory, Hampshire, c.1814, either by Jane's niece Anna Austen,
later Lefroy, or by her nephew James Edward Austen-Leigh

Private collection

12

12 Godmersham Park, Kent, 1785

Private collection

13

13 Chawton Great House, Hampshire, photographed *c*.1950

Private collection

14

14 Jane Austen's house, Chawton, Hampshire, as it looked at the time she lived there, sketched by either Anna Austen or James Edward Austen-Leigh

Private collection

15

16

Jane Austen's house as it is today, from the front (**15**) and the side (**16**)

Photographs by J.E. Hawkridge

17 The table in the dining-room of the house at Chawton
on which Jane wrote her novels

18 The bedroom at Chawton shared by Jane and Cassandra

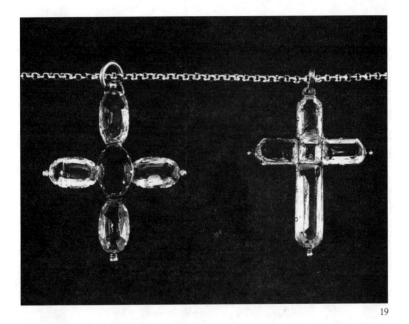

19

19 Two topaz crosses that Charles Austen gave to Jane and
Cassandra (Jane's is on the left), probably inspiring William Price's gift of an
amber cross to his sister Fanny in *Mansfield Park*

St. Michael & All Angels Cheriton

⚜ RECTORS ⚜

1210	Henry the Clerk	1517	John Foxe s.cn.l.
		1522	Walter Piers d.c.l.
		1527	John Foxe
1259	William Gauger	1530	Thomas Lupset m.a
1260	Raymond de Barinniono	1531	Robert Aldrich d.d.
		1533	Edward Leighton d.d.
		1554	Robert Aldrich d.d.
1290	William de Monte Gangeru	1558	Peter Sharp s.cn.l.
1290	John de Magnacho	1542	Edward Leighton d.d.
1292	William de Welewyck	1543	John White d.d
1297	Thomas de Bentone	1554	Stephen Whyte m.a.
1299	William de Welewyck	1572	John Bridges s.t.b.
1318	Roger de Inkepenne	1618	Richard Meredith s.d.
1319	Geoffrey de Welleforde	1622	Roger Andrewes s.t.p.
1323	William de Welewyck	1635	Francis Carter d.d.
1329	Wybert de Luttulton s.c.l.	1644	Hugh Daswell s.t.b.
1335	William de Edyngdon	1644	Heritage Darford m.a
1344	Richard de Neweburi	1661	Hugh Daswell s.t.b.
1345	Phillip de Weston	1673	William Harrison s.t.p.
1346	Peter de Inkepenne	1604	Morgan Jones m.a.
1348	John de Edyngdon	1720	Charles Trelawney m.a.
1348	John de Uske	1721	William Trimnell s.t.p.
1349	John de Edyngdon	1729	Richard Furney m.a
1351	Thomas Ffoll	1753	Robert Ashe m.a.
1351	John de Overton	1780	Edmund Ferrers m.a.
1381	John de Campeden s.cn.l.	1825	Henry Hubbard m.a.
1397	John Elmere d.c.l.	1878	Alexander Orr m.a
		1892	Alfred J.J.Cachemaille m.a
14	John Gorsuch	1894	Henry Barber
1448	Thomas Walkyngton m.a.	1904	Harold A.Brownlow s.a
1470	William Giffard s.t.p.	1945	Arthur P.Skene b.a.
1490	William Rayney s.cn.l.	1967	Roger J.D.Cholmdey b.a.
1499	Henry Sleford	1975	Eric A.Pitt o.st.j.j.,m.a.
1501	John Denby m.a.	1979	Peter McColl Robinson m.a
1508	William Thompson s.t.p.	1981	Ernest D.R.Simms m.a.b.d
1511	Gilbert at Pytte	1991	Robert E.Williams b.a.

20 A list of rectors in Cheriton Church, near Alresford, Hampshire. The incumbent from 1780 to 1825 was Edmund Ferrers, whose name perhaps bridges the gap between the clergymen Jane knew and those she created – Edmund Bertram in *Mansfield Park* and Edward Ferrars in *Sense and Sensibility*

Photograph by J.E. Hawkridge

21

21 Thomas Langlois Lefroy (1776–1869)

Private collection

22 Harris Bigg-Wither (1781–1833)

Private collection

23

23 Manydown Park, Hampshire, home of Harris Bigg-Wither

By permission of the Hampshire Record Office

24

24 The Rice Portrait. When Thomas Harding Newman gave this
to Edward Knight's grandson, John Morland Rice, he described it
as a painting of 'Jane Austen, the novelist, by Zoffany'

7

'Giving Universal Pleasure'

ANE'S comic figures are among her most successful character-
izations. Many of the best are women; but the six major works
are rich in male personalities, and there are enough unconscious
comedians to form a memorable little band, reminding the reader
of people from his or her own past, lightly pencilled though they
are. The prime specimen of *Mansfield Park*, Mr Rushworth, is also a
figure of pity, the archetypal pattern on which clowns are founded.
But clowning is foreign to Jane; her humour is always muted.

Mr Rushworth has only one moment of glory. It comes when, in
order to keep him occupied so that he shall not notice his fiancée
Maria's occupation with Crawford, he is given a sizeable part in the
private production of *Lover's Vows*.

'I am to be Count Cassel,' he announces grandly, 'and am to
come in first with a blue dress, and a pink satin cloak, and afterwards am to have another fine fancy suit, by way of a shooting-
dress.'[1] But no one is very attentive to him; they are engrossed in
the complications of casting the dramatis personae from a group of
people all beset by their own romantic problems.

At first too obtuse to notice any of the underground rumblings,
he is delighted with his task and keeps telling everyone, with great
pride, that he has two-and-forty speeches. But eventually even he

is forced to see the danger signals, and jealousy takes his mind off the work in hand. From then on

> the chances of Mr Rushworth's ever attaining to his two-and-forty speeches became much less. As to his ever making anything *tolerable* of them, nobody had the smallest idea of that, except his mother . . . the others aspired at nothing beyond his remembering the catchword, and the first line of his speech, and being able to follow the prompter through the rest.[2]

Unfortunately for him, Mr Rushworth's sole claim to Maria's affections is his twelve thousand pounds a year income and his huge mansion, Sotherton Court, which he talks frequently about engaging Repton to improve. But these material advantages fail to hold her to him once they have to compete with Crawford's dalliance. They cannot even compete in Crawford's absence. Inevitably,

> Maria, with only Mr Rushworth to attend to her, and doomed to the repeated details of his day's sport, good or bad, his boast of his dogs, his jealousy of his neighbours, his doubts of their qualifications, and his zeal after poachers, subjects which will not find their way to female feelings without some talent on one side or some attachment on the other, had missed Mr Crawford grievously . . .[3]

Mr Rushworth, sad to say, is the kind of man who would never be missed grievously by any woman except his mother; and he loses Maria.

*

In *Emma* the heroine's father, Mr Woodhouse, perhaps not so old as he seems, provides very delicate amusement. Initially lulled into feeling an almost cosy affection for him (which soon dissolves), the reader hardly likes to laugh at him outright, any more than his friends and family would have done, for every thought in his head is for other people's benefit – almost. He uses his carriage only rarely, in order to spare his coachman and horses too much labour – though, in truth, he would really far rather stay at home. He loves to entertain a few old and trusted friends – provided they leave early – but is so anxious not to give them indigestion that he cannot bear to see them eat. He is always regretful when people marry, feeling that they would have been happier single – especially when marriage has obliged them to forfeit some of the pleasures of his hearth, which he cannot conceive that they would want to do. He is courteous, chivalrous and solicitous for everyone's health and happiness and is 'everywhere beloved for the friendliness of his heart and his amiable temper . . .'[4] But even in the first flush of youth he could never have been anything but narrow, slow-witted and as tiresome to his close family as only a professional weakling can be. One wonders with every speech he makes how Emma's late mother, bright and talented as we are told she was, could have committed her future to his trembling custody.

The ruination of one little supper-party is luckily staved off by the presence of Emma, who has difficulty in contriving to be a good hostess in the face of his assiduous concern.

Such another small basin of thin gruel as his own was all that he could . . . recommend; though he might constrain himself, while the ladies were comfortably clearing the nicer things, to say:

'Mrs Bates, let me propose your venturing on one of these eggs. An egg boiled very soft is not unwholesome. Serle understands boiling an egg better than anybody. I would not recommend an egg boiled by anybody else – but you need not be afraid, they are very small, you see – one of our small eggs will not hurt you. Miss Bates, let Emma help you to a *little* bit of tart – a *very* little bit . . . I do not advise the custard. Mrs Goddard, what say you to *half* a glass of wine? A *small* half-glass, put into a tumbler of water?'[5]

The arrival of the breezy Frank Churchill into Mr Woodhouse's rarefied little world – where everyone speaks *sotto voce*, moves slowly, refrains from banging doors and handles him with the utmost care – is something of a shock to his system. 'That young man is not quite the thing,' he murmurs woefully.[6]

His opinion is confirmed soon afterwards. Frank, discussing in front of him the arrangements for a dance to be held at the Crown Inn, is reckless enough to put forward the advantages of the draughty inn as opposed to his father's warm house, by saying that no one will need to open any windows there. The dread suggestion of a window ever being opened in an over-heated assembly seems to the appalled Mr Woodhouse quite beyond belief, and he says so. Frank then indulges in a little mock gravity, which he knows will escape uncensured.

'Ah! sir – but a thoughtless young person will sometimes step behind a window-curtain, and throw up a sash, without its being suspected. I have often known it done myself.'

'Have you, indeed, sir? Bless me! I never should have supposed it. But I live out of the world, and am often astonished at what I hear.'[7]

In spite of his aversion to marriage as a state, Mr Woodhouse feels it his duty to make the traditional courtesy call on any bride arriving in Highbury. The ghastly Mrs Elton, thus newly ensconced, would have taken it as an extraordinary personal compliment, judging from her later reaction to his careful politeness; but in this case, to Mr Woodhouse's sorrow, he had not felt himself equal to the short coach ride. He is full of self-reproach, however.

'I made the best excuses I could for not having been able to wait on [Mr] and Mrs Elton on this happy occasion: I said that I hoped I *should* in the course of the summer. But I ought to have gone before. Not to wait upon a bride is very remiss. Ah! it shows what a sad invalid I am! But I do not like the corner into Vicarage Lane.'[8]

Jane in her brief life had close contact with more than one 'sad invalid' who struggled on into comparatively fit old age. One feels that Mr Woodhouse was destined (despite Jane's hints to the contrary when asked for verbal sequels by her family) to be there still, in the best armchair, tucked up beneath a soft blanket, with a screen around him, sipping thin gruel for another thirty years. But no one would have grudged him his little eccentricities, because he was so thoroughly *nice*.

*

Anne Elliot, the heroine of *Persuasion*, possesses a father of a very different kind, yet equally impossible in his contrasting brand of selfishness. The vainest man imaginable, Sir Walter Elliot is so puffed up with pride in his ancestry, his position in the world – the best that credit can buy – and his personal appearance that he is unable to carry on a normal conversation. Again the reader is driven to wonder what the heroine's departed mother saw in him, since by all accounts she was a restrained, intelligent and in every way admirable lady. When arranging marriages in the eighteenth century, one must assume that parents took no account whatever of compatibility, nor of their daughters' feelings.

Anne spends the whole of the novel in love with one particular naval officer, but Sir Walter more than redresses the balance by his horror of sailors as a breed. He condemns the Navy as a means of 'bringing persons of obscure birth into undue distinction'[9] and of ravaging the complexions of its officers by contact with sun and sea air. He recalls 'a certain Admiral Baldwin, the most deplorable looking personage you can imagine, his face the colour of mahogany, rough and rugged to the last degree, all lines and wrinkles, nine grey hairs of a side, and nothing but a dab of powder at the top'.[10] He had been quite sure that this travesty of a human being was sixty if he was a day; but to his astonishment the admiral turned out to be twenty years younger. '"It is the same with them all," Sir Walter reflects loftily. "They are all knocked about, and exposed to every climate, and every weather, till they are not fit to be seen."'[11]

He is no more gallant when the blemishes are on the opposite sex and makes so little secret of his scorn that his daughters openly discuss it. Mrs Clay, with clear designs on Sir Walter, is dismissed by his eldest daughter – cast in her father's mould – as unlikely to attract him. She sneers at Anne, who has mentioned the possibility.

'One would imagine you had never heard my father speak of her personal misfortunes, though I know you must fifty times. That tooth of hers! and those freckles! Freckles do not disgust me so very much as they do him: I have known a face not materially disfigured by a few, but he abominates them. You must have heard him notice Mrs Clay's freckles.'[12]

Freckles play only a minor part in his catalogue of abominations. Newly arrived in Bath he is struck by the number of its plain women:

One handsome face would be followed by thirty, or five-and-thirty frights; and once, as he had stood in a shop in Bond-Street, he had counted eighty-seven women go by, one after another, without there being a tolerable face among them . . . and as for the men! they were infinitely worse. Such scarecrows as the streets were full of![13]

He then dwells on the fine military figure of his friend Colonel Wallis – regrettably sandy-haired, however – and fishes very transparently for flattery from his audience which, being received, encourages him to be uncomplimentary about another of his daughters. '"How is Mary looking?" said Sir Walter, in the height of his good humour. "The last time I saw her, she had a red nose, but I hope that may not happen every day."'[14]

Sir Walter is so concerned with outward show that there is never any room in his heart for humanity or pity. When Anne declines an invitation to an elegant evening party in order to visit a past friend from her boarding-school days who has fallen on hard times, Sir Walter unleashes the full flood of his sarcastic snobbery on her:

'Who is Miss Anne Elliot to be visiting in Westgate Buildings? – A Mrs Smith. A widow Mrs Smith, – and who was her husband? One of the five thousand Mr Smiths whose names are to be met with everywhere. And what is her attraction? That she is old and sickly. Upon my word, Miss Anne Elliot, you have the most extraordinary taste! . . . But surely, you may put off this old lady till tomorrow. She is not so near her end, I presume, but that she may hope to see another day. What is her age? Forty?'[15]

It would be comforting to think that Sir Walter later receives his just deserts. But Jane lets many of her less pleasant characters off lightly, especially if they have afforded her readers amusement. So Sir Walter preens his way through the novel, untouched from beginning to end by anything worse than having to let his house to provide ready cash – unless his haughty eldest daughter's lack of a desirable match for him to enter into his family Bible can be counted as sufficiently onerous punishment.

*

Sense and Sensibility, though the work of Jane's lively youth, does not possess a man placed there expressly for us to laugh at. Its humour lies almost exclusively in the direct hands of the author or in Elinor Dashwood's silent observations. The unconscious humorists are women, notably the Steele girls and languid Lady Middleton, whose husband Sir John is, however, a mildly comic figure; he is hospitable but never selective, jolly but never witty and talkative but never worth listening to. But we learn less about him from what he says than from what Jane herself says.

For instance, when he first meets Elinor and Marianne's half-brother, 'Abundance of civilities passed on all sides. Sir John was ready to like anybody, and though Mr Dashwood did not seem to know much about horses, he soon set him down as a very good-natured fellow . . .'[16] which he was not! Some distant cousins of Lady Middleton – the Misses Steele – are discovered staying in the neighbourhood, and from then on Elinor and Marianne know no peace. 'Sir John wanted the whole family to walk to the Park directly, and look at his guests. Benevolent, philanthropic man! It was painful to him even to keep a third cousin to himself.'[17] Elinor's worst fears are realized: the Steele sisters are sly, self-seeking, ingratiating and do not even make up for these evils by being good conversationalists.

But the well-intentioned Sir John is oblivious to all this and promotes their acquaintance very busily, so that immediately

> that kind of intimacy must be submitted to which consists of sitting an hour or two together in the same room almost every day. Sir John could do no more; but he did not know that any more was required. To be together was, in his opinion, to be intimate; and while his continued schemes for their meeting were effectual, he had not a doubt of their being established friends.[18]

He embarrasses the Dashwood sisters by a lot of bluff teasing about their romances – which are progressing so badly as to be a source of distress to them both. And, once Edward Ferrars has paid Elinor a flying visit, she can never again sit at Sir John's dinner table

> without his drinking to her best affections with so much significancy and so many nods and winks as to excite general attention. The letter F had been likewise invariably brought forward, and found productive of such countless jokes, that its character as the wittiest letter in the alphabet had been long established with Elinor.[19]

Sir John, as a well-mannered gentleman and connoisseur of the arts, can be judged by his rapt attention when Marianne – a gifted musician – plays and sings for the company. He is 'loud in his admiration at the end of every song, and as loud in his conversation with the others while every song lasted'.[20] And, as a student of human nature, he can be summed up by his own summing-up of Willoughby:

> 'As good a kind of fellow as ever lived, I assure you. A very decent shot, and there is not a bolder rider in England.'

'And is *that* all you can say for him?' cried Marianne indignantly.
'But what are . . . his pursuits, his talents, and genius?'

'Sir John was rather puzzled.

'Upon my soul,' said he, 'I do not know much about him as to all *that*. But he is a pleasant, good-humoured fellow, and has got the nicest little black bitch of a pointer I ever saw.'[21]

*

In *Northanger Abbey* the most amusing man is the hero Henry Tilney, who gets his own quiet enjoyment from leg-pulling and who humours other people rather more than is perhaps good for their souls – though it is undoubtedly good for their egos. But Tilney is not a comedy character as such; like Mr Bennet of *Pride and Prejudice* we laugh with him, not at him.

John Thorpe, the loud-mouthed 'rattle', is probably the nearest Jane goes towards providing an actual male object for amusement in *Northanger Abbey*. But Thorpe is altogether too unpleasant and would, if given his head, be too crashing a bore to fill the vacancy to perfection. He is an empty-headed braggart who cannot talk about anything but

> himself and his own concerns . . . of horses which he had bought for a trifle and sold for incredible sums; of racing matches, in which his judgement had infallibly foretold the winner; of shooting parties, in which he had killed more birds . . . than all his companions together . . .[22]

Catherine Morland is only seventeen and very inexperienced, but 'she could not entirely repress a doubt, while she bore with the effusions of his endless conceit, of his being altogether completely agreeable'[23] and is courageous enough 'to distrust his powers of giving universal pleasure'[24] – with which assessment the reader is bound to concur.

*

Jane's best-known comedian, whose powers of giving universal pleasure are guaranteed, is the impossible Mr Collins of *Pride and Prejudice*. When he comes to visit his cousins the Bennets for the first time, the obloquy in which he is held by Mrs Bennet because he is due to inherit her husband's entailed estate is matched only by the overwhelmed delight with which she greets the idea of his proposal to Elizabeth. However, he is such a pompous young man, and so studied in his heavy gallantry, that not only does Elizabeth give him a refusal as firm as his rebuttal of it will allow but her father declares he would never have spoken to her again if she had accepted.

Her friend Charlotte Lucas, however, is not troubled by the prospect of having an embarrassing and over-loquacious husband, just so long as she has a husband of some sort, so she 'good-naturedly engaged Mr Collins's conversation to herself'[25] and kindly keeps him company on chilly November walks for so much of his stay that by the time he is due to go home she has agreed to become Mrs Collins. Mrs Bennet is aghast. Charlotte, the plain daughter of her dear friends Sir William and Lady Lucas, has pulled off a little coup which she never finds it in her heart to forgive.

Mr Collins, blissfully unaware of protocol, pushes himself forward at every possible opportunity. Attending a dance given by Mr Bingley at Netherfield, he is in transports of joy to find himself in the same room with a relation of his patroness Lady Catherine de Bourgh, her nephew Mr Darcy. Mr Darcy being by far the most illustrious gentleman present in the assembly, Elizabeth learns with horror that Mr Collins intends to rush in where angels fear to tread and force his company upon someone who is not renowned for his friendly warmth towards *hoi polloi* and who would, as Elizabeth knows, 'consider his addressing him without introduction as an impertinent freedom rather than a compliment to his aunt'.[26]

But there is no holding Mr Collins back and he insists:

'I am most thankful that the discovery is made in time for me to pay my respects to him, which I am now going to do, and trust he will excuse my not having done it before. My total ignorance of the connection must plead my apology . . . I consider myself more fitted by education and habitual study to decide on what is right than a young lady like yourself;' and with a low bow he left her to attack Mr Darcy, whose reception of his advances she eagerly watched, and whose astonishment at being so addressed was very evident . . . It vexed her to see him expose himself to such a man. Mr Darcy was eyeing him with unrestrained wonder; and when at last Mr Collins allowed him to speak, replied with an air of distant civility.[27]

Mr Collins, undaunted, launches into another speech, and only when positively snubbed does he return to Elizabeth's side – to her amazement, well pleased with his reception.

It is when Elizabeth goes to stay in Kent with the newly wed Mr and Mrs Collins in the vicarage at Rosings and sees her cousin in action with his patroness, an august and interfering *grande dame*, that the reader realizes to the full how lucky our heroine is to have escaped marriage with him.

The chief business of Mr Collins's life, apart from baptizing, marrying and burying his parishioners and reading sermons not only in church but to the ladies in the evenings, is to bow and scrape to Lady Catherine and her bleak young daughter. He had already confided as much to the Bennets, earnestly reporting:

'Lady Catherine herself says that, in point of true beauty, Miss de Bourgh is far superior to the handsomest of her sex; because there is that in her features which marks the young woman of distinguished birth. She is, unfortunately, of a sickly constitution, which has prevented her making that progress in many accomplishments which she could not otherwise have failed of . . . But she is perfectly amiable, and often condescends to drive by my humble abode in her little phaeton and ponies.'[28]

He is happy to add that he regularly thinks up suitable compliments to pay these great ladies, one of them being that the younger's poor state of health, in preventing her from travelling to London, 'has deprived the British Court of its brightest ornament'.[29] Another, which he has apparently employed many times, is that the charming Miss de Bourgh seemed born to be a duchess and 'the most elevated rank, instead of giving her consequence, would be adorned by her'.[30] However, Lady Catherine has other plans: to marry her daughter to Mr Darcy. Luckily he is a young man with a mind of his own and he has no designs whatever on Miss de Bourgh.

Elizabeth's first dinner invitation with the Collinses to the palatial Rosings is a mark of his patroness's kindness which Mr Collins hardly knows how to praise enough, and he stands with his watch outside the ladies' doors, calling out reminders of the time. He also decides that Elizabeth may need to be told what to wear:

'Do not make yourself uneasy, my dear cousin, about your apparel. Lady Catherine is far from requiring that elegance of dress in us which becomes herself and daughter. I would advise you merely to put on whatever of your clothes is superior to the rest; there is no occasion for anything more.'[31]

The reader would feel sorry for the silly fellow if it were not for the fact that he is really not at all kind. When Lydia Bennet elopes with Wickham and her family are plunged into mortified gloom, he writes a letter of smug triumph to Mr Bennet which instantly removes any vestige of pity he may have aroused earlier:

> Be assured my dear sir, that Mrs Collins and myself sincerely sympathise with you, and all your respectable family, in your present distress, which must be of the bitterest kind, because proceeding from a cause which no time can remove . . . The death of your daughter would have been a blessing in comparison of this. And it is the more to be lamented, because there is reason to suppose, as my dear Charlotte informs me, that this licentiousness of behaviour in your daughter has proceeded from a faulty degree of indulgence; though, at the same time, for the consolation of yourself and Mrs Bennet, I am inclined to think that her own disposition must be naturally bad . . . this false step in one daughter will be injurious to the fortunes of all the others; for who, as Lady Catherine herself condescendingly says, will connect themselves with such a family? And this consideration leads me, moreover, to reflect, with augmented satisfaction, on a certain event of last November; for had it been otherwise, I must have been involved in all your sorrow and disgrace.[32]

Later, of course, with the marriages of Elizabeth and Jane Bennet to Mr Darcy and Mr Bingley, the Bennet family rises again like a phoenix from the ashes, and the glad prospect emerges of Mr

Collins having to eat humble pie in the future. But with their escape to Mr Darcy's Derbyshire estates Elizabeth and her bridegroom would not have to suffer his attentions at very close range. The suffering is all reserved for his dear Charlotte, who seems from her remarks on Lydia's upbringing to have taken an unexpected pleasure in the Bennets' temporary misfortunes and so forfeits our sympathy, along with her husband.

8

Anti-Heroes

T HE short works and fragments do not give much scope for discussion. *Lady Susan* and *Love and Freindship* (Jane's archaic
spelling is preserved to this day) are both written as letters, and the
men hardly count. But in the unfinished works we catch illuminating
glimpses here and there. *The Watsons* promises a self-important Tom
Musgrave, while *Sanditon* does better still with Mr Parker, bounding
in his enthusiasm like an eager puppy, and the rather precious Sir
Edward Denham, who lives in a dream-world, forever carrying off
Miss Brereton to his tent. The heroes of the principal novels – or,
more correctly, the men who will marry the heroines – have a chapter
to themselves later, but there is nearly always an early period in each
book when the first-time reader feels sure that the hero is going to be
someone else. At least one of these 'false' heroes is more interesting
and lively than the real one; and they are not all quite as false in both
meanings of the word as George Wickham or John Willoughby.

Willoughby, of *Sense and Sensibility*, has such powers of physical
attraction for Marianne Dashwood that all her thoughts and
feelings are concentrated on him. She becomes a tight knot of
brooding passion, with no room in her mind for anyone or anything
else. And his persuasive effusions lead her and her warm-hearted
mother into believing that he will offer her marriage.

But neither Marianne nor her mother are very shrewd women, whereas the analytical Elinor thinks Willoughby rather too good to be true. The Dashwoods live in a Devonshire cottage which, though of reasonable comfort, in no way compares with Willoughby's own nearby inheritance, Allenham Court, nor his estate at Combe Magna in Somerset. But on one occasion they are all discussing with him the improvements Mrs Dashwood would like to make, if ever she could afford it, to which

> he warmly opposed every alteration of a place which affection had established as perfect with him.
>
> 'What!' he exclaimed, 'improve this dear cottage! No. *That* I will never consent to. Not a stone must be added to its walls, not an inch to its size, if my feelings are regarded . . . To me it is fault-less. Nay, more: I consider it as the only form of building in which happiness is attainable; and were I rich enough I would instantly pull Combe down, and build it up again in the exact plan of this cottage.'
>
> 'With dark narrow stairs, and a kitchen that smokes, I suppose,' said Elinor.[1]

When Willoughby changes, and neglects Marianne, she falls into a decline terrible in its intensity; her despair is as all-consuming as her happiness had been, and it makes her physically ill. This seems melodramatic to us now but was sadly all too common in unhappy girls then with their frustratingly walled-in lives. A 'decline', unless from actual disease, was similar perhaps to an anorectic condition; in either case, many young women died of it.

Willoughby is sorry when he sees what he has done, but one knows deep down he would never have continued to value such an easily taken prize as Marianne. (Conversely, her churlish indifference to Colonel Brandon inspires in return his ardent, unwavering devotion – a result which, though having a small element of truth in it, might be stretching credibility a fraction too far.) Willoughby's faults really revolve around his selfishness; he is the handsome womanizer who loves Marianne against his will but who loves money a great deal more. Our greatest consolation, on Marianne's behalf, is the certainty that in a very short time his transparent and gushing insincerity would have driven her into falling as firmly out of love as she had fallen into it.

In *Pride and Prejudice* sweet-smiling Wickham is a rogue who speaks 'in the gentlest of accents'[2] – he is a practised scrounger, schemer and spendthrift. He steals the hearts of all Meryton at first, until he begins to leave a few bad debts behind him when he moves to Brighton, upon which, true to form, the town is soon buzzing with the information that he had never been any good. His sins of extravagance, profligacy, ingratitude and lying are further compounded by his past attempt to abduct the fifteen-year-old Miss Darcy for her money. Apart from this unspeakable behaviour, he begins a courtship of Elizabeth Bennet, next switches to a wealthier local lady, then finally and inexplicably elopes with Lydia, as poor of course as Elizabeth and nowhere near such good company. Jane never satisfactorily explains this sudden lowering of his sights, and she grants him parole by allowing him to smile his way through potentially embarrassing Bennet family scenes later and avoid any awkward denouement. His charm is permitted to save his face after all, it seems.

*

The false hero Henry Crawford in *Mansfield Park* has a great deal more to offer by way of sex-appeal and presence than the one true light of Fanny Price's life, Edmund Bertram – except for his height.

This is the only physical attribute he noticeably lacks, and it is seized on by the man whom he eventually dishonours, Mr Rushworth. 'For my part, I can see nothing in him . . .' says Rushworth in a vain effort to keep up his creaking morale. 'Nobody can call such an under-sized man handsome. He is not five foot nine. I should not wonder if he was not more than five foot eight. I think he is an ill-looking fellow.'[3] But Rushworth is almost alone in his condemnation. His beloved but fickle Maria is head over heels in love with Crawford, her sister Julia suffers jealous pangs though she is not so deeply embroiled, the male Bertrams regard him as a worthy friend, Sir Thomas thinks he is an astoundingly fine match for Fanny – and the only other person not totally beguiled by him is Fanny herself.

Crawford is actually a rarity among Jane's gentlemen. In all her novels the action centres on the heroine and is seen from her view-point almost all the time – which is why we do not have a chance to overhear exclusively male conversations, a source of some complaint from critics. But Henry Crawford is one of the few men under whose skin we are allowed to creep briefly. When Fanny's seafaring brother William visits Mansfield Park Crawford takes a temporary back seat as the Bertram family are regaled with William's experiences of naval battles and shipwrecks – not that Jane details these herself. However, William has obviously done them justice, actually managing to elicit from dull Lady Bertram a placid 'Dear me! how disagreeable! I wonder anybody can ever go to sea.'[4]

In Crawford they produce just the right reaction.

His heart was warmed, his fancy fired, and he felt the highest respect for a lad who, before he was twenty, had gone through such bodily hardships . . . The glory of heroism, of usefulness, of exertion, of endurance, made his own habits of selfish indulgence appear in shameful contrast; and he wished he had been a William Price, distinguishing himself and working his way to fortune and consequence with so much self-respect and happy ardour, instead of what he was!

The wish was eager rather than lasting. He was roused from reverie . . . by some enquiry of Edmund as to his plans for the next day's hunting; and he found it was as well to be a man of fortune at once with horses and grooms at his command.[5]

At this stage rapport seems to be establishing itself between the reader and the villain of the piece – a dangerous situation to arise. The danger is averted when Crawford runs off with Maria and proves Fanny's judgement to be right, but one is still left with the feeling that he might have made as good a hero as not and a far more entertaining mate for Fanny than the one she chose.

David Cecil says that Henry Crawford was 'designed as a villain, came to life as a sympathetic character, and was driven back to sinful courses by an arbitrary use of his author's prerogative'.[6] Dr Chapman disagrees, arguing that Crawford's character was consistent, being made up of 'intellect, charm, and boundless good humour, tempering a cold-blooded cynical selfishness'.[7] When comparing these judgements it is perhaps worth recalling that Henry Austen, the critic closest to Jane, found his wicked namesake a clever and pleasant man – while not, we must assume, entirely approving of his morals.

*

Frank Churchill in *Emma* is the only other false hero worthy of notice, but he turns out to be rather a shallow and thoughtlessly selfish young man – quick and glib with his excuses, laughing endearingly when discovered in petty subterfuges, able to write a disarming letter to smooth away the problems he has created and winning the affections of an intelligent girl, both beautiful and dutiful, Jane Fairfax. Emma calls him the child of good fortune,[8] while Mr Knightley, unimpressed, adds that he is likely to be happier than he deserves.[9] In the end, partly because he is the son of everyone's favourite dinner-guest Mr Weston and partly because he is a good-looking young man whom the world must love since he is a lover, he escapes scot-free and no one else passes judgement on him at all.

The one truly unforgivable facet of Frank Churchill's character is his readiness to slight his fiancée – more than once in cosy conversations with the unwitting Emma – for the sake of preserving the secret of his romance and diverting suspicion into other channels. He may well be happier than he deserves. But Miss Fairfax does not seem so lucky.

*

There are many other well-drawn men in Jane's works who do not fall into any specific category. Mr Bennet of *Pride and Prejudice* is on his own, a husband who would have been well suited either to Mrs Woodhouse or Lady Elliot but is hopelessly wrong for Mrs Bennet – the definitive case where 'imbecility in females' had presumably enhanced personal charms. One would have thought Mr Bennet would always have been too sensible to let himself be taken in by a wool-brained martyr to self-centred vapours, however pretty a girl she may have been, but sadly he has condemned himself to spending the rest of his life smiling quietly at his own ironic philosophizing, with only one of his five daughters completely able to appreciate what he is talking about. He has his own faults of character, inability to get down to unpleasant tasks being one of them and open derision of his wife another, but, in the latter case at least, who could fail to make some allowances for him?

Mr Elton in *Emma*, though a churchman, is not a benevolent person. He is a social climber, vindictive and insincere, and an obsequiously effusive swain to Emma – though there is some confusion in her mind as to whom his protestations are addressed. In fact he aspires to marry her for reasons of advancement, not love. But, needless to say, the determined, managing Emma feels herself greatly superior to him. She has him in mind for her protégée Harriet Smith, sweet but silly and unfortunately illegitimate, into whose eager arms she virtually thrusts him on every available occasion, which he manages to misconstrue as encouragement from Emma herself.

Both Emma and Mr Elton are staggered and outraged on discovering each other's intentions. Thinking at first that he is drunk when he proposes to her, Emma retreats into angry hauteur:

'Mr Elton, my astonishment is much beyond anything I can express. After such behaviour as I have witnessed during the last month, to Miss Smith . . . Believe me, sir, I am far, very far, from gratified in being the object of such professions.'

'Good Heaven!' cried Mr Elton, 'what can be the meaning of this? Miss Smith! I never thought of Miss Smith in the whole course of my existence . . . I think seriously of Miss Smith! Miss Smith is a very good sort of girl: and I should be happy to see her respectably settled . . . but as for myself, I am not, I think, quite so much at a loss. I need not so totally despair of an equal alliance as to be addressing myself to Miss Smith! No, madam, my visits to Hartfield have been for yourself only; and the encouragement I received – '

'Encouragement! I give you encouragement! Sir, you have

been entirely mistaken in supposing it. I have seen you only as the admirer of my friend. In no other light could you have been more to me than a common acquaintance.'[10]

This is too much for the indignant Mr Elton to bear with equanimity, and he promptly pours balm on his shattered pride by going to Bath and finding a young and pretty wife with a comfortable little fortune of ten thousand pounds. Thus 'vanity and prudence were equally contented'.[11] And, since Mrs Elton's disposition is a caricature of his own, one can only presume that they are destined for a happy marriage.

In *Mansfield Park* there is a wider range of male types than in any of Jane's other books. At one end of the line is Fanny Price's father. When she arrives tired and hungry with her brother William to stay at her old home in Portsmouth after a decade of living in grandeur with her aunt Lady Bertram, Mr Price makes his entry by kicking aside her luggage in the hall with an oath, yelling out for a candle which is never brought, and then not noticing her when he advances into the dark little room where she is seated. He tells William in dockside tones about his ship the *Thrush* leaving harbour and shouts on interminably until William says:

'But . . . sir; here is Fanny,' turning and leading her forward; 'it is so dark you do not see her.'

With an acknowledgement that he had quite forgot her, Mr Price now received his daughter; and having given her a cordial hug, and observed that she was grown into a woman, and he supposed would be wanting a husband soon, seemed very much inclined to forget her again.

Fanny shrank back to her seat, with feelings sadly pained by his language and his smell of spirits; and he talked on only to his son, and only of the *Thrush*, though William, warmly interested though he was, in that subject, more than once tried to make his father think of Fanny, and her long absence and long journey.[12]

However, Mr Price, though well-meaning, has absolutely no breeding, a fault that certainly cannot be laid at the door of Fanny's uncle by marriage, Sir Thomas Bertram. He is equally well-meaning but grave, unbending and therefore frightening to her for much of her youth. But in the end Sir Thomas shows that he has a heart of gold, when he finds Fanny on a cold day sitting in the icy room her other aunt Mrs Norris has ordained she shall have, separated from her loftier cousins and unheated even in the depth of winter. He remains there to chide her because she will not marry Crawford, but, though furious with her, his kind sense of justice triumphs. When she next uses the room there is a fire in it ready and waiting for her.[13] From then on she fears him less and likes him more, and we know that when she eventually marries his son Edmund she will have a father-in- law more thoughtful of her comfort than her own father was.

Persuasion produces some men in the background who do not entirely run true to type. Captain Harville is an example of the typical sailor who can perform any practical tasks, a legacy of his days as a midshipman. Domesticated though he is, Harville makes us feel he would be just as capable out on the ocean, battling with the elements or the French alike. Not so his friend Captain Benwick, an emotional, easily depressed gentleman whose love of poetry would not in itself detract from his masculinity if only there were any other evidence that he is manly enough ever to have taken command of a ship. Of the three sea-captains in *Persuasion*, Wentworth and Harville are convincing; Benwick is not.

In the same way Mr William Elliot, Sir Walter's ambitious heir who briefly pays court to his cousin Anne, behaves in an unconvincing manner at the end of the novel. His earlier attentions to Anne were an exercise in pursuit of quick money and social advancement, yet he eventually finds his mate in the equally ambitious Mrs Clay, who has nothing material to offer him. Mrs Clay might well think Sir Walter's heir was the next best catch to Sir Walter himself, but Mr Elliot is surely slipping if he feels he can do no better than Mrs Clay – even though her snaggle-tooth and freckles may not arouse the same degree of repugnance in him as they do in some of his relatives.

However, a writer cannot have outstanding success with all the characters he or she creates and Jane's success, if not total, is very nearly so. She avoids wild flights of fancy in her people as well as in her situations, so that her novels have the ring of truth about them without which fiction cannot withstand changes of fashion. And Jane's fiction has endured through two centuries, when all else has altered so much that the world now seems a different planet from the one she knew.

PART IV

Romance in Fiction and Fact

9

Husbands for Heroines

THE romantic male lead of Jane's novels is personified in most readers' minds by Mr Darcy – the Pride in opposition to Elizabeth Bennet's Prejudice. Tall, handsome, wealthy, strong-willed, powerful, opinionated, aristocratic and haughty, he is quite unassailable but, fortunately for those at his mercy, a man of principle, even if he does make his own rules. So intimidating is he that Mrs Bennet plunges into ever greater depths of verbal idiocy whenever he is near, her daughters Kitty and Lydia respond to his presence with mute awe, his friend Mr Bingley is completely under his thumb, his cousin Colonel Fitzwilliam trails meekly in his wake, even Mr Bennet treats him with respect, and he renders the arrogant Caroline Bingley a nauseatingly deferential sycophant, except on those occasions when desperation makes her lose her head and show her true colours. Yet with Elizabeth Bennet he surprises us – and himself. Once he has finished swinging between icy inertia and elegantly restrained repartee, puzzling Elizabeth into her own seesaw of dislike and love, he is suddenly proved to have been a lifelong model of integrity. And though his actions were high-handed, his intentions were – most of the time – high-minded. The turnabout is complete, and Mrs Bennet sums up what many a prejudiced reader must feel for the greater part of the novel towards the proud Mr Darcy: 'Pray apologize for my having disliked him so much before. I hope he will overlook it.'[1]

Jane herself never disliked her Mr Darcy for one moment. He was the first man of star quality whom she created and she retained a soft spot for him always, as she admits in her letters. She may have liked him as a hero because her heroine could sharpen her wits on him and rely on his gallantry towards her to keep him from retaliating, which he was perfectly capable of doing. This eventually makes him satisfying to the reader too, because he has not wasted his power on puny matters but used it quietly to help Elizabeth.

Verbally, Darcy's chivalry is confined to her alone. When Miss Bingley makes several ill-advised attempts to put him off Elizabeth by pointing out her faults, he puts her in her place every time. Elizabeth walks through mud and rain to visit Netherfield, where her sister Jane is a temporary invalid, and gets her skirts and shoes dirty. Miss Bingley is disgusted at her untidy hair and muddy petticoat, visible beneath her let-down skirt. She thinks it shows 'an abominable sort of conceited independence, a most country-town indifference to decorum'.[2]

> 'I am afraid, Mr Darcy,' observed Miss Bingley, in a half-whisper, 'that this adventure has rather affected your admiration of her fine eyes.'
>
> 'Not at all,' he replied: 'they were brightened by the exercise.'[3]

Later, Elizabeth has just protested that Mr Darcy sets too high a standard in his definition of an accomplished woman and expresses doubts, with great temerity, that he ever finds any accomplished women at all. When Elizabeth has departed, Miss Bingley decides to attack her on this score:

'Eliza Bennet,' said Miss Bingley, when the door was closed on her, 'is one of those young ladies who seek to recommend themselves to the other sex by undervaluing their own, and with many men, I dare say, it succeeds; but in my opinion it is a paltry device, a very mean art.'

'Undoubtedly,' replied Darcy, to whom this remark was chiefly addressed, 'there is meanness in *all* the arts which ladies sometimes condescend to employ for captivation. Whatever bears affinity to cunning is despicable.'

Miss Bingley was not so entirely satisfied with this reply as to continue the subject.[4]

After some months they all meet again, when Elizabeth makes a summer tour of Derbyshire. Miss Bingley, despite having no encouragement, has not given up her pursuit of Mr Darcy, and makes one last forlorn attempt to diminish Elizabeth in his eyes: 'I must confess that I never could see any beauty in her.' She then goes on to catalogue Elizabeth's defects, including her thin face, dull complexion, uninteresting nose, 'tolerable' teeth and shrewish eyes. This fails to elicit any response from Mr Darcy, except for a 'somewhat nettled' look, so she makes one last onslaught:

'If I remember, when we first knew her in Hertfordshire, how amazed we all were to find that she was a reputed beauty; and I particularly recollect your saying one night . . . "*She* a beauty! I should as soon call her mother a wit." But afterwards she seemed to improve on you, and I believe you thought her rather pretty at one time.'

'Yes,' replied Darcy, who could contain himself no longer, 'but *that* was only when I first knew her; for it is many months since I have considered her as one of the handsomest women of my acquaintance.'[5]

After an unpromising start, Darcy is now Elizabeth's entirely; and – who knows? – part of her appeal may have lain in the fact that she was almost the only person whom he was unable to dominate.

*

The other main contender for the title of Jane's most romantic hero is Captain Frederick Wentworth of *Persuasion* – an equally happy choice of foil for Anne Elliot and a rather more approachable gentleman all round. His good looks and even temper are never in doubt, though his constraint towards Anne prevents these from being fully illustrated. Also, he is so lionized by the Musgrove women that he hardly needs to assert himself. No one really dislikes him as a person, but Anne's sister and father despise him for not being rich or heir to a title, and her older friend Lady Russell has preached caution and persuaded her against marrying him at nineteen years old, before the story begins. Too late, it seems, at twenty-seven Anne has realized this was a heartbreaking mistake. Frederick Wentworth has, not unreasonably, turned his back on her and forged ahead with his naval career, proving that marriage to him would have been eminently proper on all counts, as well as blissful; and, in the meantime, Anne has faded while he has flourished. But when they meet again later, the charms of younger, more shallow girls pall quickly when compared with Anne's sterling worth. Luckily it is not too late to make up for lost time, Anne by this stage being persuasible only by him.

Throughout the book, Wentworth's is a wide-open character. The only unanswered question is whom he will marry – and there is never much doubt as to what the outcome will be. Anne's other suitor, her cousin, comes on the scene too late to be a true alternative and is soon discredited, so, as a hero, Wentworth is a more obvious choice than Darcy. And in the future, beyond the 'happy ending', his brighter personality should influence the stoically subdued Anne and turn her into the most admirable of all Jane's women – a little less outspoken than Elizabeth Bennet (if one dare criticize such an object of general adulation) and far less cynical than Elinor Dashwood, Anne's only two real rivals.

*

To provide the perfect man for Jane herself, one would have to find someone as masterful, intelligent and personable as our previous two heroes with, in addition, the precisely complementary characteristics which would single him out as being right for her. While appreciating her lively ripostes, he would have to have the steady, avuncular kindness which would not allow her to get away with too much caustic wit. While being wealthy enough – and willing – to supply a home for a lonely ageing Mrs Austen or Cassandra, he must not be patronizing about the way he would do it. In fact, though gentleman-like, he must have the common touch. And above all, he must be good-humoured and sensible, for Jane could never suffer fools gladly, particularly not cross ones.

She did, as it happened, create this paragon. He was not Mr Darcy or Captain Wentworth but George Knightley, who in *Emma* possesses all the attributes that her most independent and critical heroine, Emma Woodhouse, requires in a man and which Jane herself would surely have demanded. Mr Knightley has a more rounded character than any of her other leading men, and we see more of him, in many different situations.

He plays rough games with delighted little nephews; sits a horse with serene ease while dictating, against all odds, the pattern of a conversation from street to upstairs window; walks in all weathers to evening functions without bothering to cut a dash in his carriage unless he needs it to give an invalid a lift home; takes a fatherly interest in his tenants; is kind, generous and helpful to poor old Mrs Bates and her garrulous daughter and timid Mr Woodhouse and fragile Jane Fairfax; refuses to be nettled or overridden by pushy Mrs Elton; and, though he hates dancing, is happy to tread a graceful measure when it is the means of rescuing Harriet Smith from her solitary station by the wall.

He is a natural psychologist and, though looking every inch the gentleman, is truly liberal-minded and tolerant: 'Little things do not irritate him,' says Mrs Weston.[6] Even more important, he is severe with Emma when he feels her cleverness has overstepped the bounds of good manners and yet avoids giving offence when he tells her about it. So, though never beating about the bush, his basic goodwill serves him excellently in lieu of smooth tact.

Jane endows Emma and Mr Knightley with the kind of unspoken camaraderie which would stand any married couple in good stead and which includes the ability to communicate succinctly with no need for formal trimmings. When they are among a small party at Mr and Mrs Weston's, an unexpected snowstorm blows up, giving rise to a variety of reactions among the guests: distress to Emma's feeble father and sister Isabella; terseness from Isabella's husband, who had not wanted to go visiting in the first place; and unrealistic offers of a night's lodging from the determinedly hospitable Mr Weston, to his wife's silent anguish. But there is one small island of quiet common sense among the waves of fluster:

> Mr Knightley and Emma settled it in a few brief sentences: thus:
> 'Your father will not be easy; why do you not go?'
> 'I am ready, if the others are.'
> 'Shall I ring the bell?'

'Yes, do.'

And the bell was rung, and the carriages spoken for.[7]

Emma and Mr Knightley are therefore marked out for cosy compatibility of the kind which Jane would have loved to find in a man herself but – except perhaps once – never did. Misunderstanding plays such a large part in most romantic literature, with plenty of it in the rest of Jane's works, that in *Emma*, a novel almost entirely based on misunderstandings and misconceptions in the mind of the central character, such effortless and deep-rooted rapport between this most calmly masculine of all Jane's heroes and the most self-possessed of her heroines cuts like a clean knife through the complexities of the plot. The only surprise is that, despite all the signals, Emma takes so long to find out with whom she and Mr Knightley are each really in love.

Frederick Wentworth is the handsome war hero who, twice over, can sweep Anne Elliot off her feet without even trying, and Fitzwilliam Darcy is King Cophetua to the unlikely beggar-maid of the sparkling Elizabeth Bennet. But down-to-earth George Knightley, all-wise, all-seeing, master of a large estate which prospers despite his proclivity for giving away the apple crop to less fortunate neighbours, is the one who would have made Jane happy.

*

Only one other hero of Jane's novels comes across with something of the attraction of these first three, and he is Henry Tilney of *Northanger Abbey*. He is tolerant, amusing and amiable and enjoys watching other people's interactions as much as does Jane herself. But, while he is full of life and wit in the Bath scenes, the structure of the story dictates that he is perhaps a more muted personality once he gets into his own home, the Abbey. He feels guiltily uncomfortable there, paying court to Catherine Morland because he has been ordered to by his horrid old father, who thinks Catherine is rich. General Tilney is quite the nastiest specimen of all Jane's gentlemen, which makes him the least convincing as a character. This is presumably intentional, for, as Mary Lascelles says, *Northanger Abbey* is a burlesque and General Tilney a mock villain. His unreal persona is the more startling when one considers that he has sired two pleasant children out of three – a situation which takes even less account of hereditary likelihood than the relationship between Elizabeth and Mrs Bennet, Emma and Mr Woodhouse or Anne and Sir Walter Elliot.

The fact that Henry later defies his father and continues the courtship he has begun may prove him an admirably steadfast swain, but in his final decision to make Catherine happy he is rather too similar to the stodgy Edmund Bertram of *Mansfield Park*, who apparently marries his loving and long-suffering Fanny only because she is there.

*

Edmund Bertram's only real heroic qualities are his looks. His personality lets him down for, though he is a good, conscientious man and nice to Fanny when he remembers to be, he is too easily distracted by Mary Crawford's less urgent but more alluring claims on his time. Right up to the last few pages he regards Fanny as a sort of junior sister. When she stumblingly tries to thank him for a gift (bestowed only in a fraternally kind way) by saying that she feels much more than she can possibly express, he replies, 'My dear Fanny, you feel these things a great deal too much'[8] – a most unsatisfactory attempt at response. It is only because of circumstances beyond his control that he eventually gets around to thinking of her in other terms. By then the novel has reached the epilogue stage, so we have watched the burgeoning love affair from only one angle, Fanny's.

*

Equally unheroic are the anaemic pair who ultimately wed Elinor and Marianne Dashwood in *Sense and Sensibility*. Marianne's suitor, Colonel Brandon, interested Jane as little as he interested Marianne – so little in fact that she did not bother to give him a Christian name. For most of the novel he is a shadowy figure, spending the bulk of his time mooning about and making half-declarations of vicarious love in unfinished sentences to the sister of the girl he wants. He does not even have the courage to make a gift of a living to the impoverished clergyman Edward Ferrars openly and outright, so that Elinor has to make excuses for him. 'Colonel Brandon', she says, 'is so delicate a man that he rather wished anyone to announce his intentions to Mr Ferrars than himself.'[9]

Indeed the feather-light impact of this delicate colonel would not cut much ice in the average officers' mess – even less in the line of battle. Luckily, he seems to have mislaid his regiment, as shadowy as himself, rather early for a commanding officer still in his thirties. If he had ever been forced into action with it, one dreads to think with what lugubrious hesitancy he would have led it. But, in extenuation, he proves himself a man of purpose when it really matters, becoming galvanized into life just once towards the end of the story when Marianne's illness forces him into a long and dramatic ride to fetch her mother.

Poor Elinor's Edward Ferrars is never galvanized at all. Fate carries him along like a leaf on the wind and, like Edmund Bertram, everything that happens to him is of someone else's making. 'Neither fitted by abilities nor disposition to answer the wishes of his mother or sister, who longed to see him distinguished as – they hardly knew what',[10] the best his author could say of him was that he had 'an open, affectionate heart' and that his understanding was good.[11] And he is, at least, blisteringly honest. When confronted with Marianne's poetic excesses, he says stoutly that he does not like crooked, twisted, blasted trees but prefers them tall, straight and flourishing.[12] While one cannot help warming to Edward momentarily in this tiny shaft of sensible sunlight, it is nevertheless still impossible to think of him as a heroic figure any more than Colonel Brandon.

When Elinor, everyone's intermediary, offers him on Brandon's behalf the living which will enable him to start a predictably slow climb up the ladder of ecclesiastical promotion, he is able only to *look* his gratitude, astonishment and so on, confining his spoken delight to the numbing words 'Colonel Brandon!'[13] He later admits what we have all learned by then: 'I feel it – I would express it if I could, but, as you well know, I am no orator.'[14]

These two tongue-tied gentlemen take the heroines to wife, but they both do so without any noticeable wooing or the exercise of any apparent charm. Thackeray called *Vanity Fair* a novel without a hero; Jane could well have done the same for *Sense and Sensibility*. However, perhaps the fault, with regard to Edward and Elinor at any rate, lies in the way Elinor's character is developed. Elizabeth Jenkins remarked that, as many men feel instinctively ill at ease with calmly and acutely perceptive women, 'if the portrait of her lover Edward Ferrars seems colourless and flat, one can say at least this for it: that it represents the kind of man who might reasonably be expected to fall in love with Elinor'.[15] Though hardly the case now, that was on the whole true of men until fairly recently – a very dreary cross for all acutely perceptive Elinors to have to carry!

If intentional from the outset, this situation of a novel with two heroines and no heroes could be taken as an early statement of Jane's latent feminism. If, on the other hand, it just grew naturally as the book went along, both of *Sense and Sensibility*'s leading men have to be regretfully recognized as failures.

*

Noting that Edmund Bertram and Edward Ferrars are both clergy-men, one can feel only that if familiarity did not exactly breed contempt in Jane's mind it definitely did nothing to spark inspiration. Henry Tilney is more attractive but still not inspired. The really inspired parson is the foolish Mr Collins. But oily, self-seeking Mr Elton follows hot on his heels. And there is one more example to back them up – the slothful, food-obsessed Dr Grant of *Mansfield Park*, whose existence serves merely to illustrate a point but who has no importance in his own right. However, those parsons whom Jane makes romantic leads may not be the 'vile creatures' that Cardinal Newman calls them, but they are certainly less attractive than their naval and landowner parallels in the other novels.

It may seem strange, therefore, to discover that of the men in Jane's own life whom she viewed with an eye to romance, one particular parson meant more to her than any of the officers or country gentlemen whose names might have appeared on her dance programmes. There were many flirtations, with people of varied types and occupations, but the man whom by all accounts she would have most liked to marry was a clergyman. And there was also another man of the cloth whom she openly described as a piece of perfection. But the gentleman who wanted to make her mistress of his fifteen hundred Hampshire acres had his marriage offer refused. And the only officer with whom she ever professed herself 'in love' was a writer whom she never met – a Captain Pasley who produced an entertaining book on the unlikely subject of the Military Police.[16]

10

In Search of Love

THE great love of Jane's life did not appear on the scene until she was in her middle twenties, though there were one or two false alarms and trivial romances to be encountered first. These began in earnest about five or six years earlier.

The first person who seems to have stirred Jane's adolescent emotions was Edward Taylor, a future MP for Canterbury. This youthful infatuation, however, was short-lived; her later delight at the prospect of his marriage to his cousin Charlotte – which never actually took place – is evidence enough of that. While staying in Kent in 1796 she passed his home, a gracious manor house, and wrote to Cassandra: 'We went by Bifrons, & I contemplated with a melancholy pleasure, the abode of Him, on whom I once fondly doated.'[1]

The real business of life and romance began later, at the New Year following Jane's twentieth birthday. It was a riot of social comings and goings as usual, and her letter of 9 January 1796 flings us immediately into the heart of the mêlée at the Harwood family's ball at Deane House, as she dances twice with Mr John Willing Warren, once with Mr Charles Watkins

and, to my inexpressible astonishment, I entirely escaped John Lyford. I was forced to fight hard for it, however. We had a very

good supper, and the greenhouse was illuminated in a very elegant
manner . . . I wish Charles had been at Manydown, because he
would have given you some description of my friend, and I think
you must be impatient to hear something about him.[2]

The friend is really the focal point of the letter, much of the rest
being mere background detail, setting the scene at the dance. In
pride of place stood an Irishman, Thomas Langlois Lefroy, blue-
eyed, auburn-haired, handsome and just twenty, having celebrated
his birthday the day before. A law student of Trinity College,
Dublin, he was the nephew of the Rector of Ashe (and thus
nephew-in-law of Jane's older friend Mrs Lefroy) and he was
staying with them on holiday.

By the night of the Harwood ball Jane had decided that she
might fall in love with Tom and felt that he was more than a little in
love with her, so she was on tenterhooks wondering if he would
declare himself.

She had no hesitation in regaling Cassandra with light-hearted
details of the romance she had embarked on because Cassandra
was engaged at the time to the Reverend Thomas Fowle, a cousin
of the Lloyd sisters. And someone who is in love herself is the
easiest person to write to about one's own love affair. There is no
fear of making the reader envious of one's happiness and very little
dread of earning reproofs for recklessness or over-exuberance. But
Jane was apparently not completely safe from Cassandra's
reproachful pen, even then. 'You scold me so much,' Jane said,

in the nice long letter which I have this moment received from
you, that I am almost afraid to tell you how my Irish friend and I
behaved. Imagine to yourself everything most profligate and
shocking in the way of dancing and sitting down together. I *can*

expose myself, however, only *once more*, because he leaves the country soon after next Friday, on which day we *are* to have a dance at Ashe after all. He is a very gentlemanlike, good-looking, pleasant young man, I assure you. But as to our having ever met, except at the three last balls, I cannot say much; for he is so excessively laughed at about me at Ashe, that he is ashamed of coming to Steventon, and ran away when we called on Mrs Lefroy a few days ago.[3]

Jane had achieved a substantial victory in getting Tom Lefroy to attach himself at all, however lightly, since, though when he was at Trinity he had won three gold medals for debating, he was, paradoxically, shy and quiet in company. He covered up this defect like many shy people – and perhaps like Mr Darcy, whom Jane brought into the world ten months later – with a slightly haughty manner.

He seems to have been overworking at his law studies and on the verge of breakdown. The ubiquitous 'nerves' and his eyes gave him trouble and he failed to get the fellowship that had been expected of him. His London-based great-uncle, Benjamin Langlois, came to the rescue and Tom decided on the strength of this that he might like to study law in London instead.[4] To supply the brief rest cure first, who were more suitable than Benjamin's nephew and niece-in-law, the Lefroys of Ashe? Unfortunately for Jane perhaps, they were right on her doorstep and Mrs Lefroy was one of her closest friends.

He went into these new surroundings at the deep end. Debating society medals were no help among the brittle, cliquey English gentry celebrating Christmas and the New Year with their dances and parties. He withdrew into silence. Park Honan suggests that at this point some of the mute shyness which was so noticeable during his stay at Ashe could be put down to uncertainty at the reception an Irish accent might receive in these rarefied assemblies. He certainly did not seem to move comfortably among the happy throng, though he was not ashamed, as Jane had said, of coming to Steventon but interested enough in her to pay her a morning call with his cousin George in tow for propriety's sake.

Mrs Lefroy may have joined hollowly in the laughter at Ashe about the effect her young friend had on her husband's nephew (and indeed the flirtation was apparently the subject of some discussion among their set), but in reality she regarded it as no laughing matter at all. Tom had a brilliant legal career ahead of him but at this stage no money. If Jane had been wealthy it would have been a match worth promoting, but she was not, so Mrs Lefroy decided to nip it in the bud. (It requires considerable will-power to resist seeing Lady Russell of *Persuasion* at work here, on this occasion acting herself instead of prompting the action and having the interests of the man in mind rather than the woman. Incidentally, Mr Lefroy's predecessor at Ashe had been a Dr Russell, Mary Russell Mitford's grandfather.) In any event, Tom's departure, a rather swifter one than Jane could have wished for, was hastened by Mrs Lefroy's efforts.

But there was still a week to go before saying goodbye and Jane made the most of it, probably not at this stage aware of any undercurrents. 'After I had written the above,' she went on in her letter to Cassandra, 'we received a visit from Mr Tom Lefroy . . . he has but *one* fault, which time will, I trust, entirely remove – it is that his morning coat is a great deal too light.'5

The promised dance at Ashe was on 15 January. On the 14th Jane wrote:

I look forward with great impatience to it, as I rather expect to receive an offer from my friend in the course of the evening. I shall refuse him, however, unless he promises to give away his white Coat . . . How impertinent you are to write to me about Tom, as if I had not opportunities of hearing from him myself. The *last* letter that I received from him was dated friday the 8th . . . Tell Mary [Mary Lloyd, not yet married to James] that I make over Mr Heartley & all his Estate to her for her sole use and Benefit in future, & not only him, but all my other Admirers into the bargain wherever she can find them, even the kiss which C. Powlett wanted to give me, as I mean to confine myself in future to Mr Tom Lefroy, for whom I donot care sixpence. Assure her also as a last & indubitable proof of Warren's indifference to me, that he actually drew that Gentleman's picture for me, & delivered it to me without a Sigh.[6]

The three men of the last paragraph, Mr Heartley, the Reverend Charles Powlett and Mr Warren, had been Jane's recent escorts and, though in case of disappointment she safeguarded her self-esteem by placing on record the statement that she did not care sixpence for Tom, she had obviously made it all too clear to the others that she cared far less for them – a little rashly, as it turned out.

The morning of that last dance dawned and she could not resist putting a postscript to the previous day's letter before sending it off. 'At length the Day is come on which I am to flirt my last with Tom Lefroy, & when you receive this it will be over – My tears flow as I write, at the melancholy idea.'[7]

But she was covering up her feelings again, confident that she would 'receive an offer'. The offer did not come and Tom went back to Ireland in silence.

Just as Anne Elliot stayed friendly with Lady Russell, Jane stayed friendly with Mrs Lefroy. But they did not talk about Tom any more. When Jane is condemned for over-emphasizing the importance of money in marriage, it is perhaps forgotten that she had every reason to be uncomfortably aware of this importance as a basic fact of life, having been an early victim of it herself.

Nearly two years later, Mrs Lefroy was visiting the Austen family after a period when Tom had presumably been at Ashe again without seeing Jane. Jane waited quietly for news, but

> of her nephew she said nothing at all . . . She did not once mention the name of [Tom] to *me*, and I was too proud to make any enquiries; but on my father's afterwards asking where he was, I learnt that he was gone back to London in his way to Ireland, where he is called to the Bar and means to practise.[8]

All hope of reviving the romance with Tom had fled by then, of course. She tried to make it seem that it had not been very much more than a lightweight flirtation, conducted mainly for effect. But surely she must have been just a little in love with him or pride would not have inhibited her from asking about him.

Tom Lefroy later married Mary Paul, daughter of a rich Irish baronet, and in 1852 became Chief Justice of Ireland. He lived to be ninety-three and when asked in 1868, the year before his death, if he had ever been in love with Jane, he admitted that he had. 'But it was a boyish love,' he said.

*

The year 1796 must have seemed flat and anti-climactic after Tom's departure. The escorts left behind, whom Jane had so carelessly consigned to Mary Lloyd, were no substitute. Of Mr Heartley little appears to be known, but Jane described John Willing Warren as ugly, though he had a pleasant nature,[9] and the Reverend Charles Powlett was very small and his limbs were 'not well formed'. Jane had clearly edged away from the kiss Charles tried to give her while Tom Lefroy was monopolizing her attention. Fortunately, he was not unduly thin-skinned and, like another clerical gentleman, the rebuffed Mr Elton of *Emma*, he soon showed his powers of recovery later that year by marrying Anne Temple, daughter of a Cornish vicar.[10] Clergyman's wife and clergy-man's daughter notwithstanding, she was never destined to distinguish herself by good works in the parish but only to live for ever in Jane's letters for her expensive but 'naked' taste in clothing. In December 1798 Jane made it finally clear how she felt about the Powletts, airily writing to Cassandra that Charles 'gave a dance on Thursday, to the great disturbance of all his neighbours, of course, who, you know, take a most lively interest in the state of his finances, and live in hopes of his being soon ruined'.[11]

*

Charles Fowle was a rather different gentleman. No one seems to have suggested that he failed the basic tests of being pleasant to talk to and presentable in appearance. Furthermore, he was the younger brother of Thomas Fowle, the man to whom Cassandra, during this year of 1796, was engaged. That engagement was to end tragically; the following year Thomas accompanied his kinsman Lord Craven on Sir Ralph Abercromby's military expedition to the West Indies, but he caught yellow fever there and died.

The Fowle brothers, sons of the Reverend Thomas Fowle, vicar of Kintbury in Berkshire, had known the Austen sisters for many years, both of them having been Mr Austen's pupils. Thrown together as Charles and Jane were, it was not surprising that there would be some rapport between them. In this case the attraction seems likely to have been only on one side, Charles's, as Jane took time to shake off the impact on her life of Tom Lefroy. He was in fact the 'Charles' whom Jane had wished was at the Harwoods' ball, to give an unbiased description of Tom to Cassandra.[12] But she liked him as a friend in his own right, telling Cassandra 'I was very much disappointed at not seeing Charles Fowle of the party, as I had previously heard of his being invited.'[13]

She felt sufficiently at ease with Charles to ask him to buy some silk stockings for her, provided that they would not be too costly. In the event they were, but he went ahead and bought them nevertheless. Jane was stunned that this no doubt perplexed young man, let loose among the embarrassing mysteries of purchasing women's underwear, should take it upon himself to decide for her, and she wrote to Cassandra, 'What a good-for-nothing fellow Charles is to bespeak the stockings – I hope he will be too hot all the rest of his life for it!'[14]

However, his shopping prowess clearly improved during the next three years, with the purchase in 1799 of a fashionable Egyptian-style 'Mamalouc cap' for James's wife Mary, which Jane was not above borrowing for a ball at Kempshott Park.[15] By this time Charles Fowle was surely well on the way to being a model for Henry Tilney of *Northanger Abbey*, who amazes all the ladies at the Bath Assembly Rooms by his knowledge of sartorial details as well as comparative costs. He says breezily:

'My sister has often trusted me in the choice of a gown. I bought one for her the other day, and it was pronounced to be a prodigious bargain by every lady who saw it. I gave but five shillings a yard for it, and a true Indian muslin.'

Mrs Allen was quite struck by his genius. 'Men commonly take so little notice of those things,' said she. 'I can never get Mr Allen to know one of my gowns from another. You must be a great comfort to your sister, sir.'[16]

Poor Charles Fowle did not have a very long life, though his end was less sudden than his brother's. After studying for the Bar at Lincoln's Inn he married Honoria Townsend of Newbury in 1799 and practised there as a barrister. He also joined the Hungerford Volunteer Infantry and became the Major Commandant, for this was the start of a period when Britain was under intermittent threat of invasion by Napoleon. But in 1805 he became ill and went to Bath in the hope of a cure. Within a month or two, early in 1806, he died. He and Jane had always remained good friends.[17]

One other man who might possibly have figured in Jane's affectionate thoughts at this time was Harry Digweed, the gentle-man by whom she had wished her father's old servant John Bond could be employed when the Austens moved to Bath. Jane's aunt, Mrs Leigh Perrot, suspected that she was attracted to a Mr Digweed, and certainly in 1798 she had referred to him in a letter as her 'dear Harry'. But then she was also on cosy terms with his brother James, whom she met at dances, so perhaps it might even have been the second Mr Digweed who had caught Mrs Leigh Perrot's speculative eye.

*

Mrs Lefroy, meanwhile, had not finished with Jane. Some time before the autumn of 1798 Jane had met the Reverend Samuel Blackall, Fellow of Emmanuel College, Cambridge, who was well known to the Lefroys. Blackall was a large, imposing personage with a booming voice which he was a fraction too prone to using for instruction even when nowhere near the lecture halls. Aged twenty-eight, he was looking for a wife and was clearly attracted to Jane, but he belonged to that category of man who automatically talked down to young women on the assumption that they were generally rather stupid. However, this was such customary behaviour in Jane's day that she was only mildly put out by it. Most of her women friends would have taken it utterly for granted and not let it disturb them at all, but then they did not subscribe to Jane's independent views. Despite this one little fault, Jane liked him and listened eagerly when, on the same occasion as Mrs Lefroy failed to refer of her own free will to Tom Lefroy, she volunteered instead a morsel of news about Samuel Blackall. 'She showed me a letter which she had received from her friend [Samuel] a few weeks ago . . .' Jane told Cassandra,

> towards the end of which was a sentence to this effect: 'I am very sorry to hear of Mrs Austen's illness. It would give me particular pleasure to have an opportunity of improving my acquaintance with that family – with a hope of creating to myself a nearer interest. But at present I cannot indulge any expectation of it.' This is rational enough; there is less love and more sense in it than sometimes appeared before, and I am very well satisfied. It will all go on exceedingly well, and decline away in a very reasonable manner. There seems no likelihood of his coming into Hampshire this Christmas, and it is therefore most probable that our indifference will soon be mutual, unless his regard, which appeared to spring from knowing nothing of me at first, is best supported by never seeing me. Mrs Lefroy made no remarks on the letter, nor did she indeed say anything about him as relative to me. Perhaps she thinks she has said too much already.[18]

Margaret Llewelyn, analysing this episode in *Jane Austen: A Character Study*, comments that the last sentence seems to imply a second piece of interference in Jane's love-life by Mrs Lefroy and that she may have been adding insult to injury by triumphantly showing her a letter to prove it.[19] Yet might not the opposite be equally likely? Mrs Lefroy, having got her nephew-in-law out of what she saw as Jane's clutches, could perhaps have decided to try to compensate by promoting a romance elsewhere. Confronted with evidence that it had cooled, she might show that evidence to Jane to put her on guard against further disappointment. But she would have to do so in silence – for, after all, at that point what could she possibly say without making matters even worse?

Jane had once more kept her pride intact by handling the situation in three sentences which would have done credit to Elizabeth Bennet herself. Fourteen years later, when Samuel was vicar of North Cadbury in Somerset, he at last found his wife. Jane mentioned it the following July to Frank, serving on the *Elephant* in the Baltic:

> I wonder whether you happened to see Mr Blackall's marriage in the Papers last Janry. *We* did . . . He was married at Clifton to a Miss Lewis . . . I should very much like to know what sort of a Woman she is. He was a peice of Perfection, noisy Perfection himself which I always recollect with regard . . . I would wish Miss Lewis to be of a silent turn & rather ignorant, but naturally intelligent & wishing to learn; – fond of cold veal pies, green tea in the afternoon, & a green window blind at night.[20]

One cannot help wondering if Samuel were addicted to veal pies and green tea. The green window blind at night seems doomed to be a permanent mystery; family letters containing private humour are sometimes impossible for outsiders to fathom, and this may be a case in point.

Was Jane hoping that the new Mrs Blackall would be an admirable foil for Samuel, with his propensity for patronizing captive audiences, and that her silent ignorance would suit him on the one hand, as well as her basic intelligence and desire to be lectured on the other? Of all the imaginary virtues Jane bestows on this unknown woman, she herself possesses only one, intelligence. She knows, and she is letting Frank know too, that she would have not been the right partner for Samuel Blackall.

However, her forthright declaration on the subject of his perfection may have led Mrs Catherine Hubback, one of Frank's daughters, to the false conclusion that Samuel Blackall was the one man Jane really loved. When asked in 1870 to give her opinion on the subject of Jane's romantic entanglements, Mrs Hubback said, 'If ever she *was* in love it was with Dr Blackall (I think that was the name) whom they met at some watering-place shortly before they settled at Chawton . . . There is no doubt she admired him extremely.'[21]

The timing here could not actually apply to Samuel, whom Jane had met in her Steventon days, eleven years before Chawton. And this, as well as other ways in which Jane's mystery lover has been confused with Samuel Blackall, only goes to prove how even the most literate and sensible of families get their facts wrong once a story has to pass to a generation with no first-hand knowledge of events.

There was a little postscript, however. Though Catherine Hubback was born after Jane's death, she was quite close to Cassandra, who told her that in about 1832 she happened to meet Samuel again when on a holiday excursion to the Wye with Charles and his family. Cassandra, forgetting how time had flown, was disappointed to find him 'stout, red-faced and middle-aged – very different from their youthful hero'. So both sisters clearly did 'admire him extremely'. But admiration is not the same as love.

*

The mystery man with whom Samuel Blackall has often been confused is not known by name, and Dr Chapman, quoting Caroline Austen, calls the brief friendship he and Jane shared the nameless and dateless romance.[22] But yet the date does seem to have been fixed by Jane's surviving relatives fairly precisely as the summer when she was twenty-five.

In James Edward's *Memoir* he refers to it discreetly and anonymously, complying with the wishes of Cassandra, who divulged it only in a limited way towards the end of her life. He states that though he does not know details of name, date or place, he has it on sufficient authority not to doubt its truth. Cassandra told him, he says, that

> while staying at some seaside place, they became acquainted with a gentleman, whose charm of person, mind and manners was such that Cassandra thought him worthy to possess and likely to win her sister's love. When they parted, he expressed his intention of soon seeing them again; and Cassandra felt no doubt as to his motives. But they never again met. Within a short time they heard of his sudden death. I believe that, if Jane ever loved, it was this unnamed gentleman; but the acquaintance had been short, and I am unable to say whether her feelings were of such a nature as to affect her happiness.[23]

James Edward's sister Caroline supplied some information too.

> During the few years my grandfather lived at Bath, he went in the summer with his wife and daughters to *some* sea-side . . . and in Devonshire an acquaintance was made with some very charming man – I never heard Aunt Cassandra speak of anyone else with

such admiration – she had no doubt that a mutual attachment was in progress between him and her sister. They parted – but he made it plain that he should seek them out again – and shortly afterwards he died.[24]

Their half-sister Anna's daughter, Mrs Louisa Bellas, added her contribution, stating the date and location as the summer of 1801 and the town of Sidmouth, where

> they made acquaintance with a young clergyman when visiting his brother, who was one of the doctors of the town. He and Jane fell in love with each other, and when the Austens left he asked to be allowed to join them again further on in their tour, and the permission was given. But instead of his arriving as expected they received a letter announcing his death. In Aunt Cassandra's memory he lived as one of the most charming persons she had known, worthy even in her eyes of Aunt Jane.[25]

It is easy to see why Frank's daughter Catherine Hubback had thought that this young man and Samuel Blackall were one and the same. Not only had Jane described him to Frank as perfection but Samuel came from Devonshire too, and he did have a brother who was a doctor, practising first in Exeter, then in Totnes. However, this may not be too significant; Mrs Hubback might not be the only person to get a few facts wrong. As Louisa Bellas was Jane's great-niece and far removed from personal knowledge of her, perhaps she, too, had become confused and grafted the known doctor in Samuel Blackall's family on to the unknown family of the Sidmouth suitor. The chance that this suitor could actually be another clergyman called Blackall – an extra brother of Samuel and the doctor – is wrecked by the fact that, though these Blackalls did possess other brothers, they either died young or survived well beyond 1801. And of course Samuel himself lived too long and had known Jane too early to be the man concerned.[26]

Readers looking for Jane's lost love sometimes see him in Frederick Wentworth of *Persuasion*. They may be right. Burying delicate issues carefully as always, she might choose to cloak her clergyman in the safe disguise of a captain's uniform, free then to give rein in her last complete work to the happy ending which had in reality been withheld from her.

This feeling that the unknown lover was a dashing naval officer rather than a more staid character of the cloth inspired two strange departures from realism in the search for his identity, mentioned, and naturally dismissed as most unlikely, by George Holbert Tucker. One of these theories is better known than the other.

The writer Constance Pilgrim produced a book some years ago in which she put forward a suggestion that the poet Wordsworth's younger brother John was the man in question. But there seems no valid argument in support of this theory, and it has never been taken up elsewhere as a reasonable possibility.

Even more fantastic was an idea once voiced by Sir Francis Doyle and Ursula Mayow that in 1802 or 1803 the Austens went on a trip to Switzerland – on the subject of which they were amazingly reticent for ever afterwards – and encountered a naval officer with whom Jane fell in love, as he did with her. He was due, like themselves, to make his way later to Chamonix over the French border and agreed to meet them there. They went by separate roads, apparently, his being a more tortuous one over higher mountains. But he never arrived in Chamonix, wearing himself out and dying of brain fever *en route*.[27]

This astonishing suggestion has very little to recommend it as a solution and still leaves the poor man nameless and more or less dateless. Why, in any case, would the family switch the location of Jane's great romance to comparatively humdrum Devonshire, if it could have been set in the more picturesque environs of the Alps?

Whatever the truth of the matter, none of Jane's correspondence seems to have survived between the dates of 26 May 1801 and 14 September 1804. That May, immediately prior to the trip to Devonshire, she had written blithely about a Bath friend, Mr Evelyn, who seemed chiefly renowned for his knowledge of horse-flesh. She hoped he would take her on a trip in his phaeton in the countryside around Bath. But this was not quite as straightforward as it appeared. Mr Evelyn, though lent spurious respectability by being a Kent acquaintance of Edward's, was nevertheless in Bath officially with his wife. Worse still, he was the dreaded man who had compromised the 'adulteress' Miss Twisleton.[28]

Jane was determined to go on this outing if she could and assured the watchful Mrs Leigh Perrot – worried about her niece's reputation – that Mr Evelyn was harmless, stating that 'he gets Groundsel for his birds & all that'.[29] Mrs Leigh Perrot was silenced, if unconvinced – especially as when they first met two years earlier Jane had bluntly called Mr Evelyn a Yahoo.[30]

The outing went ahead, however, and his experience of horses served her in good stead. He drove her on a delightful trip to Kings-down in his 'very bewitching Phaeton & four' and returned her home satisfied and unsullied.[31]

After her happy letter describing this excursion, she is suddenly swallowed up in a dark tunnel of silence for over three years, until she emerges once more into the daylight in September 1804, on holiday at Lyme, where she appears on the surface to have resumed life where she left off:

Nobody asked me the first two dances – the two next I danced
with Mr Crawford – & had I chosen to stay longer might have
danced with Mr Granville . . . or with a new, odd looking Man who
had been eyeing me for some time, & at last without any introduction asked me if I meant to dance again . . .[32]

11

Retraction and Refusal

Bath and Lyme – which Jane used to visit while living in Bath – are associated with her in many people's minds. However, as the settings for her own personal sadness they would have seemed to her, on the whole, rather sad places in themselves. She must still have continued to write to Cassandra when they were apart, but now the letters had something in them which Cassandra did not want to preserve, either for her own peace of mind, since she too had known the shock of sudden bereavement when looking forward to reunion instead, or because Jane for once had laid down her innermost soul for inspection, in Cassandra's close guardianship. Not only are there no letters from Jane to show us how she felt at this time but no novels either.

Since she had committed to paper *Pride and Prejudice*, *Sense and Sensibility* and *Northanger Abbey*, there was a pause of over twelve years until she began *Mansfield Park* in 1811, and the only works she attempted in that time were the abandoned fragment *The Watsons* and the rewritten *Lady Susan*, originally produced in 1793–4. Her mood was wrong for writing; and it was wrong for enjoying herself, as five years of letters from 1804 show. It had also been wrong, during that earlier silent period, even for making decisions.

In the autumn of 1802 Jane and Cassandra left Bath for a visit to James and Mary at Steventon, and on 25 November they arrived to stay a few days with Alethea and Catherine Bigg at Manydown Park near Wootton St Lawrence, about three miles west of Basingstoke.

Manydown Park was an interesting old mansion built around a square court, from which its tall exterior windows looked out over impressive grounds, sheltered and softened by shrubberies. Inside, it was not one of the fine modern buildings such as the elegant young people at Mansfield Park thought so desirable, for its dark-wainscotted rooms included a hall where the Court Leet had been held since medieval times. Much of the building was therefore pre-Tudor and was steeped in history – that of one family, the Withers, a daughter of which had married a Bigg and brought about a change in the family name. The lands attached to this old house were considerable, covering seven local parishes as well as two – Wymering and Widley – towards the coast. Some of this, in Jane's day and earlier, was forested, and timber from Manydown Park had been used for part of the roof and nave of Winchester Cathedral.[1]

The home of which Jane might have become mistress was not ostentatious, yet it wore an air of established grandeur. It was not fashionable, but it had comfort and grace to recommend it and familiarity, too, for it had been a base for the Austen sisters' social life since they were young girls, with Alethea and Catherine and their now widowed sister Elizabeth Heathcote – living there with her little son – all long-term friends. Alethea and Catherine, particularly, had figured frequently in Jane's letters as companions and sometimes hostesses at parties and balls. They were lively, sociable girls in whose company Jane and Cassandra felt relaxed and happy. Their younger brother Harris, aged twenty-one, was heir to the Manydown estates.

The father of this family was Mr Lovelace Bigg-Wither, a widower with a broad and genial manner to match a broad and genial face framed with white hair. He was benevolent outside as well as inside the home and had taken his duties as deputy lieutenant for Hampshire – a post he had held nearly ten years earlier – very seriously. As Jane commented once when he was taken ill and caused an emergency which ruined a local ball: 'Poor man! . . . his life is so useful, his character so respectable and worthy, that I really believe there was a good deal of sincerity in the general concern expressed on his account.'[2]

The combination of Bigg and Wither as a surname was comparatively new, and the daughters of the house continued to use the single name, Bigg. Lovelace and his son, however, adopted the double-barrelled version, though both men added to the confusion by occasionally being known as Wither alone.

Harris was the second son of the family, but his elder brother had died and Harris was thrust into the position of heir. He was afflicted with a stammer – a frustrating condition for a youth with three bright sisters – and during his childhood two tutors had worked hard at trying fruitlessly to correct this problem, one hopes with a degree of tolerance ahead of their time. As a young man he went up to Worcester College, Oxford, from where he emerged with one of the characteristics of Samuel Blackall and another of Tom Lefroy: he wanted to display his erudition, yet, with good reason, he was also rather shy. Shy men seemed drawn to Jane, who was probably never at a loss for the right words to bring out the best in them. But Harris and his father both tended to forget that brevity is the soul of wit, and Jane admitted to being a little irritated by this.[3] Halting speech can sound ponderous and pedantic if the speaker is determined to have his say, which may well have distressed both Harris and his audience. He could at times be moody and tactless, neither of which defects would have made him a joy to live with, yet, coming from an amiable family as he did, there must surely have been some hereditary virtues to balance these minor flaws.

Jane's niece Caroline Austen, whose parents knew Harris, described him as a fine, well-built man, but plain and awkward in manner, sometimes even uncouth.[4] Many very young men are awkward and uncouth, of course, but they generally improve with age. Whether or not these were permanent traits in Harris's case hardly affected the issue, since Jane was seeing him at his immature worst – six years her junior and unlikely at that stage to attract her.

On 2 December Harris asked her to marry him. How much warning she actually had is doubtful. The signs are always there well in advance if one is looking for them; but when a woman's thoughts are far removed from the man on the spot a marriage proposal can come out of the blue as an enormous surprise. Jane, clearly taken aback, thought first of the material advantages, not only to herself but to her mother and Cassandra in the future. Harris was an excellent match from this viewpoint and, even if she might never find a soul mate in him, she got on well with his sisters, who would probably continue to live at Manydown when she became its mistress. As Caroline – not yet born at this momentous time, but obviously having heard the tale told and re-told – felt with the hindsight of middle age that most women with Jane's precarious financial prospects would have agreed to marry Harris and hope to love him later.[5] Caroline seems, incidentally, to have revised her earlier judgement of Harris somewhat, presenting him in a more lovable light after all. Mercenary though her opinions now sound, in the climate of their day Jane could have felt the same, and feared she would do a positive disservice to everybody by refusing him. She accepted.

During a sleepless night she had second thoughts as the full realization began to dawn on her of what marriage to Harris meant on a personal scale. She knew she could never go through with it after all, and early the next morning she steeled herself to tell Harris she had changed her mind.

The exit from Manydown was precipitant, tearful and embarrassing in the extreme. Jane hastened with Cassandra to Steventon to be consoled by Mary and James, who, while they were as upset as the Manydown family by the whole humiliating episode and would have liked Jane to marry Harris, were both very supportive. Even the somewhat maligned Mary played as kindly a role as Cassandra and James, despite the fact that she could hardly believe her sister-in-law had been given such a Heaven-sent opportunity to keep up the family fortunes and had thrown it all away in this unseemly haste. Mary thought the match would have been a 'most desirable' one and reacted to the episode with 'sorrow'. In this she was probably in tune with the rest of the family for once.

At Jane's request, James took the carriage and drove the sisters straight back to Bath, which gave Jane ample time to reflect gloomily on how she had distanced herself from friends whom she liked and had hurt the feelings of poor Harris and all his family. She had also damaged the prospects of her own women relatives if they should be left without Mr Austen's protection – which before very long they were.

Alethea and Catherine did in fact stay friendly with the Austen women but not surprisingly seem to have had closer contact from then on with Cassandra rather than Jane. Two years later Harris married Anne Howe Frith, the daughter of a lieutenant-colonel in the North Hampshire militia, and they subsequently had ten children. For the first few years of the marriage they lived at

Quidhampton, where, as Mrs Lefroy reported, all the neighbourhood was pleased with the bride.[6]

*

The silent years incubated what might well have become another proposal of marriage for Jane, had she not smothered it at birth. Throughout her twenties, from 1796 to 1805, the Reverend Edward Bridges crops up in occasional letters of hers as a single man who pays more attention to her than basic politeness demands. Edward Bridges was the fifth son of Sir Brook Bridges of Goodnestone, near Canterbury, and brother of Elizabeth Bridges who had married Jane's brother Edward. He was in a very similar situation to Tom Lefroy – attracted to Jane and yet requiring in his family's eyes a wealthier wife than he could have found among the Austens.

In September 1796 Jane was staying with her brother and sister-in-law at their first marital home, Rowling. They all visited Lady Bridges for dinner and a 'Ball' (of five couples!), where they danced 'two Country Dances & the Boulangeries'. And there Edward Bridges chose to open the dancing with Jane – a mark of his private liking and quite an honour as well.[7]

A long if spasmodic friendship ensued and Jane progressed from being 't'other Miss Austen',[8] his original name for her, to someone considerably more important. Nine years later, in the August of 1805, on another visit to Goodnestone Jane was still writing with amused pleasure about Edward's courtesy and care of her. 'We were agreeably surprised by Edward Bridges's company . . . It is impossible to do justice to the hospitality of his attentions towards me; he made a point of ordering toasted cheese for supper entirely on my account.'[9]

Some time around this period it seems that Edward decided to ask Jane to marry him, or at any rate he began a conversation with her which sounded like a preamble to a proposal. Jane had not forgotten the recent débâcle at Manydown, nor the past reaction of an anxious aunt when Tom Lefroy looked as if he would fall victim to Jane's charms. She did not want to make an enemy of Lady Bridges, who was very kindly disposed to her as Elizabeth's sister-in-law but who would not have welcomed a closer relationship. Acceptance or refusal of Edward's suit would be equally disastrous for different reasons – acceptance because Jane did not love him (and she knew that, as he was a fifth son, there was no great fortune offered to make her decision a matter of duty towards Mrs Austen and Cassandra) and refusal because it would be hurtful and ungracious. Once bitten, twice shy; and this time she was too quick to be caught out. She stopped – or diverted – the proposal in midstream and she managed it cleverly enough to keep friendship alive.

Writing later with reference to an invitation Lady Bridges extended to Cassandra, Jane said, 'I wish you may be able to accept Lady Bridges's invitation, tho' I could not her son Edward's; – she is a nice Woman . . .'[10]

In 1809 Edward Bridges married Harriet Foote, a sister of his eldest brother's wife Eleanor (who was apparently much pleasanter than Harriet). 'I wish him happy with all my heart,' declared Jane when she heard of the engagement,

> & hope his choice may turn out according to his own expec-
> tations, & beyond those of his Family – And I dare say it will.
> Marriage is a great Improver – & in a similar situation Harriet may
> be as amiable as Eleanor . . . When you see him again, pray give
> him our Congratulations & best wishes.[11]

But Harriet was a disappointment. Writing to Frank at sea,

Jane called her 'a poor Honey – the sort of woman who gives me the idea of being determined never to be well – & who likes her spasms & nervousness & the consequence they give her, better than anything else'. Then she regretted having said it, and added, 'This is an illnatured sentiment to send all over the Baltic!'[12]

She maintained a gentle interest in Edward Bridges to the last, speaking of him in October 1813, when she was at Godmersham again:

> We have had another of Edward Bridges' Sunday visits. – I think the pleasantest part of his married Life, must be the Dinners & Breakfasts & Luncheons & Billiards that he gets in this way at Gm. Poor Wretch! He is quite the Dregs of the Family as to Luck.[13]

*

Later years did not produce any September romances, though on Jane's arrival at Chawton she found Mrs Knight hoping she would marry the vicar Mr Papillon. Jane was amused. 'I *will* marry Mr Papillon,' she said obligingly, 'whatever may be his reluctance or my own. – I owe her much more than such a trifling sacrifice.'[14] In the event, it was Henry who ultimately married Mr Papillon's niece Eleanor Jackson.

Eighteen months before Jane's death we get a glimpse of the last man to be, if not in love with her, impressed. The Reverend James Stanier Clarke, Chaplain to the Prince of Wales – and he who had escorted her around Carlton House Library and later tried to direct her writing into more august channels connected with the House of Coburg – wrote her an effusive letter in December 1815, though not the kind which would have recommended him greatly to his 'dear Madam'.

On Monday I go to Lord Egremonts at Petworth – where your Praises have long been sounded as they ought to be . . . You were very good to send me Emma – which I have in no respect deserved. It is gone to the Prince Regent. I have read only a few Pages which I very much admired – there is so much nature – and excellent description of Character . . .

Then, duty done, he changed course and suggested that she should write a novel about a clergyman forced by an unsympathetic High Priest of the Parish to bury his own mother before going to sea 'as the Friend of some distinguished Naval Character about a Court'.[15]

Brian Southam remarks that Clarke was 'set upon literary immortality' and was offering the experiences of his own life as a chaplain in the Navy and at court for inclusion in Jane's work – as well as airing some personal resentment towards his late mother's parish priest. His keen interest was therefore not entirely objective.

After sowing these seeds, as he hoped, Clarke begged forgiveness for constantly

wishing to elicit your Genius; – & I fear I cannot do that, without trespassing on your Patience and Good Nature . . .Pray, dear Madam, remember, that besides My Cell at Carlton House, I have another which Dr Barne procured for me at No. 37, Golden Square – where I often hide myself. There is a small Library there much at your Service – and if you can make the Cell render you any service as a sort of Half-way House, when you come to Town – I shall be most happy. There is a Maid Servant of mine always there.[16]

So Jane would not have needed to keep her hand on the lock of the door during the length of her sojourn at 'the cell', as she had felt impelled to do with Mr Holder in the drawing-room at Ashe Park! A comforting last sentence from a harmless man but one who was not destined to be on Jane's short-list of favourite gentlemen.

*

There are no other Austen papers extant which refer to men wanting to marry Jane; but there is a firm and long-standing tradition in his family that Thomas Harding Newman of Nelmes, near Hornchurch, Essex, proposed to her by letter. Originally Thomas Harding, he took the further name of Newman, his grandmother's maiden name, in 1808, on the death of his father Richard Harding Newman, and this style was subsequently adopted by the heirs to Nelmes.

A wealthy gentleman who also inherited Clacton Hall, Essex, and Black Callerton, Northumberland, from his maternal uncle, and whose forebears had possessed estates in Jamaica and Barbados,[17] Thomas hunted with his own pack of foxhounds, travelled widely and, being an excellent shot, was a welcome guest at many a great house. Though he may have lived principally in Essex, he had connections in the West Country and no doubt paid the usual fashionable visits to Bath, where he perhaps met Jane. (Some members of his family, at least, were on familiar ground in Bath: in 1829 his first cousin John Harding married Elizabeth Taylor at Walcot Church, where Jane's parents had been married and her father was buried.)[18]

Thomas may, alternatively, have made Jane's acquaintance through the Lefroys, who were probably known to him, since in 1841 his younger son Benjamin married Anne Lefroy Sadleir.[19] Her mother Elizabeth was Tom Lefroy's sister and thus niece to the Lefroys of Ashe and cousin to their children Ben Lefroy – Anna

Austen's husband – and Mrs Lucy Rice.[20] Lucy Rice's son married Edward Knight's daughter Elizabeth, and this was the branch of the Austen family to receive the Rice portrait from Thomas's elder son Dr Thomas Harding Newman, Fellow of Magdalen, not long before he died in 1882.[21]

As well as the Lefroy connection of the next generation, there is another group of people that could link Jane and the Harding Newmans – the Barne family of Sotterley and Dunwich, Suffolk. In James Stanier Clarke's letter to Jane offering her the use of his Golden Square cell when she came to London, he said, in passing, that it was procured for him by Dr Barne, mentioning this fellow-clergyman as if Jane knew him. One does not casually bring in an unnecessary reference to a third person, as he did, unless that person is known to both the writer and recipient of the letter. (The mention of Lord Egremont at Petworth earlier in the same letter had a dual purpose, that of name-dropping and paying a compliment to Jane, neither of them applicable to Dr Barne's reference.)

Dr Thomas Barne was Chaplain-in-Ordinary to George III, George IV and William IV, and his sister Sarah was married to Thomas Harding Newman's uncle, John Harding.[22]

John and Sarah Harding's only son, John, was on friendly terms with his first cousin and, being a keen diarist, not only recorded a few useful genealogical details among his entries, he also related a story of later years, when he took a yacht from Torquay to Exmouth where Thomas Harding Newman came on board. They stayed at Ivybridge overnight, then John sailed alone to Spitswick. On arrival, the cousins changed places. Thomas had ridden his black gelding to meet the yacht, so John rode the horse back to Ivybridge while Thomas took back the boat.[23] Thomas and John were obviously good friends and this could be a possible means by which Jane, who it seems clear knew John's uncle, Dr Barne, could have met Thomas.

Tenuous links though these connections with the Lefroy and Barne families might appear individually, added together they produce weight for the case that Jane Austen might well have encountered Thomas Harding Newman at some brief point in her life and received another sadly unwelcome marriage proposal. Though it has never been substantiated by any documents found in Austen records, with no letters discovered in which Jane mentioned Thomas's name, this fact cannot in itself constitute grounds for dismissing the legend. His social background and that of his descendants – many of them members of that most practical of professions, the Army – make it most unlikely for a story of being spurned by Jane Austen to have been remembered throughout the generations unless it were true.

Unfortunately for him, the archetypal hunting-and-shooting gentleman was clearly never of great romantic interest to Jane, especially if his timing was unlucky. And it would appear that Thomas came on the scene, like Harris Bigg-Wither, soon after her one great disappointment in love. Born in November 1779, Thomas was nearly four years Jane's junior and then in his early twenties. He was married three times: in 1810 to Harriet Cartwright of Ixworth Abbey and Bucklesham Hall, Suffolk; then to Elizabeth Hall of Holly Bush, Derbyshire; and lastly to Anna Parry of Donnington Priory, Berkshire. He died at Speen, Berkshire, in 1856.[24]

The feeling among his descendants that Thomas Harding Newman had wished to marry Jane is naturally strengthened by his family's past possession of the Rice portrait. It would be a logical assumption that while Mrs Elizabeth Harding Newman was given it by one of the Austens partly because she admired Jane's novels, this may not have been the only reason for the gift. With no descendants of Jane's to inherit it, who could be a more suitable trustee than one of the ladies who had accepted the offer Jane rejected? And surely no one was better suited to receive it later than Thomas's heir. Finally, that heir saw fit to return it to Edward Knight's grandson, John Morland Rice, whom he had known at Oxford, and he described it in his accompanying letter, dated 30 December 1880, as a painting of 'Jane Austen, the novelist, by Zoffany'.[25]

*

For a woman who never married, Jane's mind dwelt frequently on the subject of wedlock. From her earliest girlhood days she invented bridegrooms for herself, and once she entered them in the specimen pages on her father's parish register – those pages laid out to help the bride, groom and witnesses to see where to place their signatures or marks. She filled these with mock marriages of her own, the names of the spouses unfortunately being fictitious, such as Jack Smith of Nowhere or Edmund Arthur William Mortimer of Liverpool.

Her thoughts may have lingered imaginatively on marriage and quality of love, but in real life she dealt very briskly with love of an unrequited sort. Her opinion of a romance which fell through or was one-sided was stated in unequivocal terms in a letter to Fanny Knight: 'it is no creed of mine . . . that such sort of Disappointments kill anybody.'[26] Nevertheless, she always lent a sympathetic ear whenever anything of the kind threatened her beloved Fanny's composure, and Fanny was the person who drew forth most of Jane's best-known aphorisms on love and married bliss.

In one piece of advice past discomfiture rears its head briefly, yet does not distract her aim, to be decisively honest. 'The unpleasantness of appearing fickle is certainly great – but . . .

nothing can be compared to the misery of being bound *without* Love, bound to one, & preferring another.'[27]

On a different occasion she draws again on what must be her own experience, from two aspects:

Single Women have a dreadful propensity for being poor – which is one very strong argument in favour of Matrimony, but I need not dwell on such arguments with *you*, pretty Dear, you do not want inclination. – Well, I shall say, as I have often said before, Do not be in a hurry; depend upon it, the right Man will come at last; you will in the course of the next two or three years, meet with somebody . . . who will so completely attach you, that you will feel you never really loved before.[28]

And, she might have added sadly to herself: You will also feel you can never really love again.

Though to this niece Jane could write so freely about love, she had to add her statutory sprinkling of irony to keep the subject light. She was embarrassed by emotional display to a degree which must have made the hypocrisies of social life difficult for her at times. 'I have had a most affectionate letter from Buller,' she told Cassandra in November 1800; 'I was afraid he would oppress me by his felicity & his love for his Wife, but this is not the case; he calls her simply Anna without any angelic embellishments, for which I respect & wish him happy . . .'[29] The use of the word 'respect' here is significant. Emotionalism was at best a weakness, and at worst an empty parade.

But when she was genuinely in love herself, one must believe that the most damaging elements of this restraint – Jane's sole area of inarticulacy – were cured, if only temporarily. Woman's ability to love, as expressed by Anne Elliot in *Persuasion* – and so frequently quoted that only its unique relevance excuses its presence yet again below – proves that Jane had crossed that vital threshold of feeling, once at least.

Yet life had to go on, so no emotional watershed could be allowed to affect her permanently. And in the future, once the sadness of what-might-have-been had dulled, she would realize that while it only takes an hour to discover the affinity between two mutually attracted people, more time might have shown up incompatibility. Jane knew her nameless and dateless man long enough to be in love with him, and, as it was his death and not his indifference which had snatched him away, she could afford to indulge that love for a while and to indulge the sorrow she felt. But common sense would prevail in the end and point out to her the unlikelihood of everything having remained, lifelong, as idyllic as it had been on that happy summer holiday in Sidmouth. From then on she would be able to take up a balanced, cheerful life again – wiser and only a little sadder.

Men and romance interested Jane, but as a general rule the idea of the sameness of married life seemed to depress her. She could continue to write romantic stories well after the point where she would have ceased to inspire romance herself and had reached an age where maternal interests absorbed the thoughts of most of her female contemporaries. Motherhood and baby care, however, had no appeal for Jane, merely creating further inhibitions regarding the married state. It was more comfortable to go on dwelling in the realms of fictional romance. It is not hard to see why Jane refused to do what nine out of ten women in her position would have unhesitatingly done and marry for security rather than love. She preferred to be mistress of her own thoughts and actions and was content with her own company. And it is no reflection on her personality to say that the men whom she refused were probably happier with the women whom they did marry than they would have been with her. Jane as a loving wife would have no doubt been a delight; but, where she did not truly love, she could not have dissembled sufficiently to carry off the kind of charade in which millions of married women then lived out their lives.

While Jane's familiarity with romance is never really questioned, she has often been accused of dealing with that romance on too shallow a scale because she knows little of real love. Charlotte Brontë complained of Jane: 'She ruffles her reader by nothing vehement, disturbs him by nothing profound. The passions are perfectly unknown to her.'[30] Charlotte must have missed the point of a great many profound truths in Jane's quiet irony; her own idea of desirable profundity and a correct level of vehement ruffling is to distress her readers at the end of what promise to be wholly delightful novels with grisly surprises. One of her heroes is blighted at the eleventh hour by mutilation and blindness and another is dashed to death in a shipwreck on the last page.Charlotte, determined to revert like many Victorians to the Gothic mood – and, in her own style, outstandingly successful – found the serenity of Jane's happy endings too much for her tormented spirit to bear.

She is not alone in her opinions, though others are less dramatic in their comments. Mary Lascelles says of Jane's lovers, 'Away they walk, into their private cloud, leaving us, mere eavesdroppers, behind them.'[31] The implication is invariably that Jane does not know how to deal with love scenes. On the face of it, this seems a valid point, but it is not unexpected, surely. Jane had received more than one marriage proposal of her own, but she had been in love only once, and then with a man whose overtures had not reached the stage of declaration, so she was following her known precepts on Bath and the Foresters in not advancing ideas as to how matters might go if a really welcome proposal were made.

In any event, to the accusation of passions being unknown to

Jane there is a foolproof answer – the famous lines from *Persuasion*, spoken by Anne Elliot to Captain Harville:

> Man is more robust than woman, but he is not longer lived; which exactly explains my view of the nature of their attachments . . . God forbid that I should undervalue the warm and faithful feelings of any of my fellow-creatures. I should deserve utter contempt if I dared to suppose that true attachment and constancy were known only by woman. No, I believe you capable of everything great and good in your married lives. I believe you equal to every important exertion, and to every domestic forbearance, so long as – if I may be allowed the expression, so long as you have an object. I mean, while the woman you love lives, and lives for you. All the privilege I claim for my own sex (it is not a very enviable one, you need not covet it) is that of loving longest, when existence or when hope is gone.[32]

This being a romantic novel with a happy ending, these words were luckily overheard by Captain Wentworth, who thus knew himself to be loved and who promptly righted all misunderstandings. But the heartache in that speech of Anne's lingers on the air, beyond the confines of the novel's pages. Almost all Jane's biographers draw attention to it because it is the clearest spoken expression of her understanding of love and her experience of its sorrows.

But there is ample evidence in all her works that, despite that element of feminism in her nature upon which we all seize nowadays, and despite a shy reluctance to describe passionate or intimate scenes – a procedure fraught with pitfalls yet deemed statutory by later generations of romantic writers – she knew and revelled in love's happiness, too. Fortunately for posterity, she has left it on record for the world to share.

Notes

Editions of printed sources are as listed in the Select Bibliography on page 193

CHAPTER 1

1 *Pride and Prejudice*, Chapter LVI, para. 9.

2 Marghanita Laski, *Jane Austen and Her World*, Chapter 1.

3 Letter 25, 8–9 November 1800.

4 David Waldron Smithers, *Jane Austen in Kent*, p. 99.

5 Caroline Austen, *My Aunt Jane Austen*, p. 5.

6 Caroline Austen, *My Aunt Jane Austen*, p. 8.

7 James Edward Austen-Leigh, *A Memoir of Jane Austen*, Chapter 5.

8 Letter 87, 15–16 September 1813.

9 David Cecil, *A Portrait of Jane Austen*, p. 65.

10 R.W. Chapman, *Facts and Problems*, p. 108.

11 Austen-Leigh, Chapter 12.

12 *Northanger Abbey*, Chapter XIV, paras 28–9.

13 *Northanger Abbey*, Chapter XXV, para. 24.

14 *Mansfield Park*, Chapter XVI, para. 27.

15 Letter 35, 5–6 May 1801.

16 Letter 24, 1 November 1800.

17 Letter 36, 12–13 May 1801.

18 Letter 145, 8–9 September 1816.

CHAPTER 2

1 Austen-Leigh, Chapter 1.

2 Chapman, p. 95.

3 Caroline Austen, *My Aunt Jane Austen*, p. 5.

4 Letter 67, 30 January 1809.

5 Introduction, p. xlii, to *Letters of Jane Austen*, Oxford University Press 1932, ed. R.W. Chapman; extract quoted originally published in *Transactions of the Royal Society of Literature: Essays by Divers Hands VIII*, 1928.

6 Letter 53, 20–22 June 1808.

7 Letter 10, 27–8 October 1798.

8 Chapman, p. 92.

9 Letter 30, 8–9 January 1801.

10 Letter 63, 27–8 December 1808.

11 Letter 67, 30 January 1809.

12 Letter 39, 14 September 1804.

13 *Mansfield Park*, Chapter VI, para. 49.

14 *Sense and Sensibility*, Chapter XIII, para. 57.

15 Letter 36, 12–13 May 1801.

16 Letter 30, 8–9 January 1801.

17 Letter 50, 8–9 Febuary 1807.

18 Letter 84, 20 May 1813.

19 Letter 65, 17–18 January 1809.

20 Letter 66, 24 January 1809.

21 Letter 56, 1–2 October 1808.

22 Letter 151, 20–21 February 1817.

23 Letter 155, 23–5 March 1817.

24 Laski, Chapter I.

25 *Sanditon*, Chapter VII, para. 23.

26 *Sanditon*, Chapter VII, para. 24.

27 Letter 94, 26 October 1813.

28 Margaret Wilson, *Almost Another*

Sister, pp. 110–11.
29 Chapman, p. 212.
30 Jane Austen, *The History of England*, Chapter 'Elizabeth'.
31 Jane Austen, *The History of England*, Chapter 'Mary'.
32 Madeleine Marsh, *Collected Reports of the Jane Austen Society, 1976–85*, p. 353, 'Ozias Humphry and the Austens of Sevenoaks' and 'The Portrait'.
33 Letter 13, 1–2 December 1798.
34 Winchester City Council, *Jane Austen's Winchester*.
35 Letter CEA/1, 20 July 1817.

CHAPTER 3

1 Austen-Leigh, Chapter 10.
2 Maggie Lane, *Jane Austen's Family Through Five Generations*, p. 103.
3 Letter 40, 21 January 1805.
4 Letter 41, 22 January 1805.
5 Photograph of Mathew portrait, Jane Austen Memorial Trust.
6 Caroline Austen, *Reminiscences*, p. 29.
7 Letter 55, 30 June–1 July 1808.
8 Park Honan, *Jane Austen: Her Life*, p. 233.
9 Letter 10, 27–8 October 1798.
10 Letter 50, 8–9 February 1807.
11 Elizabeth Jenkins, *Jane Austen*, Chapter XIII.
12 George Sawtell, *Collected Reports of the Jane Austen Society, 1976–85*, p. 304, 'Neither Rich Nor Handsome'.
13 Letter 146, 16–17 December 1816.
14 Letter 146.
15 Letter 160, 27 May 1817.
16 Letter 15, 24–6 December 1798.
17 Letter 10, 27–8 October 1798.
18 Letter 60, 24–5 October 1808.
19 Letter 60.

20 Letter 95, 3 November 1813.
21 Letter 90, 25 September 1813.
22 Letter 151, 20–21 February 1817.
23 Letter 13, 1–2 December 1798.
24 Letter 149, 23 January 1817.
25 Letters 87, 15–16 September 1813; and 88, 16 September 1813.
26 Letter 106, 2 September 1814.
27 Letter 51, 20–22 February 1807.
28 Letter 149, 23 January 1817.
29 Letter 121, 17–18 October 1815.

CHAPTER 4

1 Letter 70, 18–20 April 1811.
2 Letter 72, 30 April 1811.
3 Letter 71, 25 April 1811.
4 Letter 71.
5 Letter 84, 20 May 1813.
6 Letter 84.
7 *Emma*, Chapter XLII, para. 35.
8 *Emma*, Chapter XLII, para. 38.
9 Letter 86, 3–6 July 1813.
10 Letter 86.
11 *Emma*, Chapter XI, para. 26.
12 Letter 97, 2–3 March 1814.
13 Letter 121, 17–18 October 1815.
14 Letter 121.
15 Letter 121.
16 Letter 121.
17 Letter 128, 26 November 1815.
18 Letter 128.
19 Letter 82, 16 February 1813.
20 Letter 138A, 27 March 1816.
21 Letter 138D, 1 April 1816.
22 Letter 92, 14–15 October 1813.

CHAPTER 5

1 Letter 16, 28 December 1798.
2 Margaret Llewelyn, *Jane Austen: A Character Study*, p. 154.
3 Jenkins, Chapter XII.

4   Llewelyn, p. 154.
5   Letter 45, 24 August 1805.
6   Letter 51, 20–22 February 1807.
7   Letter 4, 1 September 1796.
8   Chapman, p. 125. Originally J.H. Hubback (in *Cornhill Magazine*, July 1928).
9   *Persuasion*, Chapter XI, para. 18.
10 Letter 90, 25 September 1813.
11 Letter 24, 1 November 1800.
12 Jane Austen, *The History of England*, Chapter 'Elizabeth'.
13 Letter 91, 11–12 October 1813.
14 Letter 86, 3–6 July 1813.
15 Lane, p. 158
16 Letter 18, 21–3 January 1799.
17 Letter 17, 8–9 January 1799.
18 Letter 27, 20–21 November 1800.
19 Both topaz crosses held by Jane Austen Memorial Trust.
20 Letter 38, 26–7 May 1801.
21 *Mansfield Park*, Chapter XXVI, para. 8.
22 *Mansfield Park*, Chapter XXVII, para. 2.
23 *Mansfield Park*, Chapter XXV, para. 54.
24 *Mansfield Park*, Chapter XXV, para. 55.
25 Letter 14, 18–19 December 1798.
26 Letter 15, 24–6 December 1798.
27 Letter 15.
28 Lane, p. 154.
29 Silhouette, Jane Austen Memorial Trust.
30 Letter 92, 14–15 October 1813.
31 Letter 86, 3–6 July 1813.
32 Letter 92, 14–15 October 1813.
33 Letter 92.
34 Letter 148, 8 January 1817.
35 Letter 92, 14–15 October 1813.
36 Letter 145, 8–9 September 1816.
37 Lane, p. 186.

38 Llewelyn, p. 157.
39 Mary Lascelles, *Jane Austen and Her Art*, p. 117.
40 Lascelles, p. 121.
41 Letter 104, 10–18 August 1814.
42 Entry in diary of Sir Walter Scott, 14 March 1826. Photocopy held by Jane Austen Memorial Trust; original in Pierpont Morgan Library, New York, Accession No. MA 441-42.

CHAPTER 6

1   Letter 1, 9–10 January 1796.
2   Letter 95, 3 November 1813.
3   Letter 129, 2 December 1815.
4   Letter 128, 26 November 1815.
5   Letter 129, 2 December 1815.
6   Letter 92, 14–15 October 1813.
7   Letter 17, 8–9 January 1799.
8   Letter 15, 24–6 December 1798.
9   Letter 31, 14–16 January 1801.
10 Letter 25, 8–9 November 1800.
11 Letter 33, 25 January 1801.
12 Letter 27, 20–21 November 1800.
13 Letter 20, 2 June 1799.
14 Letter 36, 12–13 May 1801.
15 Letter 56, 1–2 October 1808.
16 Letter 91, 11–12 October 1813.
17 Letter 92, 14–15 October 1813.
18 Letter 63, 27–8 December 1808.
19 Letter 10, 27–8 October 1798.
20 Letter 22, 19 June 1799.
21 Letter 25, 8–9 November 1800.
22 Letter 105, 23–4 August 1814.
23 Letter 78, 24 January 1813.
24 Letter 27, 20–21 November 1800.
25 Letter 38, 26–7 May 1801.
26 Letter 61, 20 November 1808.
27 Letter 21, 11 June 1799.
28 Letter 50, 8–9 February 1807.
29 Letter 30, 8–9 January 1801.
30 Letter 44, 21–3 April 1805.

31 Letter 60, 24–5 October 1808.
32 Letter 90, 25 September 1813.
33 Letter 109, 18–20 November 1814.
34 Letter 109.
35 Letter 109.
36 Letter 109.
37 Letter 109.
38 Letter 151, 20–21 February 1817.
39 Letter 151.
40 Letter 25, 8–9 November 1800.
41 Letter 53, 20–22 June 1808.
42 Letter 54, 26 June 1808.
43 Letter 53, 20–22 June 1808.
44 Letter 54, 26 June 1808.
45 Letter 94, 26 October 1813.
46 *Emma*, Chapter XI, para. 5.
47 *Sense and Sensibility*, Chapter XX, paras 2, 27, 39.
48 Letter 29, 3–5 January 1801.
49 Letter 39, 14 September 1804.

CHAPTER 7

1 *Mansfield Park*, Chapter XV, para. 3.
2 *Mansfield Park*, Chapter XVIII, para. 4.
3 *Mansfield Park*, Chapter XII, para. 4.
4 *Emma*, Chapter I, para. 8.
5 *Emma*, Chapter III, paras 13–14.
6 *Emma*, Chapter XXIX, para. 11.
7 *Emma*, Chapter XXIX, paras 31–2.
8 *Emma*, Chapter XXXII, para. 54.
9 *Persuasion*, Chapter III, para. 16.
10 *Persuasion*, Chapter III, para. 16.
11 *Persuasion*, Chapter III, para. 16.
12 *Persuasion*, Chapter V, para. 14.
13 *Persuasion*, Chapter XV, para. 13.
14 *Persuasion*, Chpter XV, para. 14.
15 *Persuasion*, Chapter XVII, para. 15.
16 *Sense and Sensibility*, Chapter XXXIII, para. 52.
17 *Sense and Sensibility*, Chapter XXI, para. 3.

18 *Sense and Sensibility*, Chapter XXI, para. 33.
19 *Sense and Sensibility*, Chapter XXI, para. 36.
20 *Sense and Sensibility*, Chapter VII, para. ult.
21 *Sense and Sensibility*, Chapter IX, paras 17–20.
22 *Northanger Abbey*, Chapter IX, para. 31.
23 *Northanger Abbey*, Chapter IX, para. 32.
24 *Northanger Abbey*, Chapter IX, para. 32.
25 *Pride and Prejudice*, Chapter XVIII, para. 73.
26 *Pride and Prejudice*, Chapter XVIII, para. 60.
27 *Pride and Prejudice*, Chapter XVIII, paras 57, 61.
28 *Pride and Prejudice*, Chapter XIV, para. 7.
29 *Pride and Prejudice*, Chapter XIV, para. 9.
30 *Pride and Prejudice*, Chapter XIV, para. 9.
31 *Pride and Prejudice*, Chapter XXIX, para. 5.
32 *Pride and Prejudice*, Chapter XLVIII, para. 11.

CHAPTER 8

1 *Sense and Sensibility*, Chapter XIV, paras 7–12.
2 *Pride and Prejudice*, Chapter XLI, para. 38.
3 *Mansfield Park*, Chapter X, paras 40–42.
4 *Mansfield Park*, Chapter XXIV, para. 21.
5 *Mansfield Park*, Chapter XXIV, paras 22–3.

6 Chapman, p. 195.
7 Chapman, p. 195.
8 *Emma*, Chapter LI, para. 28.
9 *Emma*, Chapter LI, para. 28.
10 *Emma*, Chapter XV, paras 31–7.
11 *Emma* , Chapter XXII, para. 4.
12 *Mansfield Park*, Chapter XXXVIII, paras 21–3.
13 *Mansfield Park*, Chapter XXXII, para. 4 *et seq.*

CHAPTER 9

1 *Pride and Prejudice*, Chapter LIX, para. 43.
2 *Pride and Prejudice*, Chapter VIII, para. 10.
3 *Pride and Prejudice*, Chapter VIII, paras 12–13.
4 *Pride and Prejudice*, Chapter VIII, paras 56–8.
5 *Pride and Prejudice*, Chapter XLV, paras 13–18.
6 *Emma*, Chapter XXVI, para. 79.
7 *Emma* , Chapter XV, paras 17–22.
8 *Mansfield Park*, Chapter XXVII, para. 9.
9 *Sense and Sensibility*, Chapter XL, para. 19.
10 *Sense and Sensibility*, Chapter III, para. 6.
11 *Sense and Sensibility*, Chapter III, para. 6.
12 *Sense and Sensibility*, Chapter XVIII, para. 8.
13 *Sense and Sensibility*, Chapter XL, para. 30.
14 *Sense and Sensibility*, Chapter XL, para. 34.
15 Jenkins, Chapter VI.
16 Letter 78, 24 January 1813.

CHAPTER 10

1 Letter 6, 15–16 September 1796.
2 Letter 1, 9–10 January 1796.
3 Letter 1.
4 Honan, pp. 106–7.
5 Letter 1, 9–10 January 1796.
6 Letter 2, 14–15 January 1796.
7 Letter 2.
8 Letter 11, 17–18 November 1798.
9 George Holbert Tucker, *Jane Austen the Woman*, p. 53.
10 Tucker, p. 54.
11 Letter 13, 1–2 December 1798.
12 Honan, p. 109.
13 Letter 1, 9–10 January 1796.
14 Letter 2, 14–15 January 1796.
15 Letter 17, 8–9 January 1799.
16 *Northanger Abbey*, Chapter III, paras 38–9.
17 Tucker, p. 53.
18 Letter 11, 17–18 November 1798.
19 Llewelyn, p. 68.
20 Letter 86, 3–6 July 1813.
21 Chapman, p. 62.
22 Chapman, p. 63.
23 Austen-Leigh, Chapter 2.
24 Chapman, p. 66.
25 Chapman, p. 64.
26 Llewelyn, p. 65.
27 Tucker, pp. 64–5.
28 Honan, pp. 173–4.
29 Letter 38, 26–7 May 1801.
30 Letter 22, 19 June 1799.
31 Letter 38, 26–7 May 1801.
32 Letter 39, 14 September 1804.

CHAPTER 11

1 Honan, p. 192.
2 Letter 18, 21–3 January 1799.
3 Honan, p. 192.
4 Honan, referring to MS Austen.
5 Honan, referring to Caroline Austen,

Frog Firle, 17 June [1870].

6 Honan, pp. 189–90.

7 Letter 5, 5 September 1796.

8 Letter 15, 24–6 December 1798.

9 Letter 46, 27 August 1805.

10 Letter 57, 7–9 October 1808.

11 Letter 61, 20 November 1808.

12 Letter 90, 25 September 1813.

13 Letter 94, 26 October 1813.

14 Letter 62, 9 December 1808.

15 Letter 132A, 21 December 1815.

16 Letter 132A.

17 Burke's *Landed Gentry*, 1965, p. 469.

18 Harding Newman family papers
    (unpublished), by kind permission of
    the late Mrs Diana M. Kleyn.

19 Burke's *Landed Gentry*, 1965, p. 469.

20 Genealogy of the Lefroys of
    Carrigglas, Burke's *Irish Family
    Records*, 1976.

21 Marsh, *Collected Reports of the Jane
    Austen Society,1976–85*, p. 353.

22 Burke's *Landed Gentry*, 1833, Vol. I,
    p. 141; and Harding Newman papers.

23 Harding Newman papers.

24 Burke's *Landed Gentry*, 1965, p. 469;
    and Harding Newman papers.

25 Marsh, *Collected Reports of the Jane
    Austen Society, 1976–85*, p. 353.

26 Letter 109, 18–20 November 1814.

27 Letter 114, 30 November 1814.

28 Letter 153, 13 March 1817.

29 Letter 25, 8–9 November 1800.

30 Lascelles, p. 119.

31 Lascelles, p. 126.

32 *Persuasion*, Chapter XXIII, paras 23,
    32.

Select Bibliography

Manuscript sources, most of them later published, consist of documents, portraits and letters, principally written by members of the Austen family, in Jane Austen's House, Chawton, Hampshire; also the unpublished papers and genealogical table of the family of Thomas Harding Newman, of Nelmes and Clacton Hall, Essex, examined when they were in the possession of the late Mrs Diana Kleyn (née Harding) of Frimley, Surrey.

Austen, Caroline, My Aunt Jane Austen, Jane Austen Society, 1991

Austen, Caroline, Reminiscences, with an introduction by Deirdre Le Faye, Jane Austen Society, 1986

Austen, Jane, The History of England, from Love and Freindship and Other Early Works, Women's Press: London, 1978

Austen, Jane, Letters, collected and edited by Deirdre Le Faye, Oxford: Oxford University Press, 1995

Austen-Leigh, James Edward, A Memoir of Jane Austen, privately published, 1871

Bowden, Jean K., Jane Austen's House, Norwich: Jarrold Publishing and the Jane Austen Memorial Trust, 1996

Burke, Irish Family Records, London: Burke's Peerage, 1976

Burke, Landed Gentry, London: Burke's Peerage, 1838 and 1965

Cecil, David, A Portrait of Jane Austen, London: Constable, 1978

Chapman, R.W., Jane Austen: Facts and Problems, Oxford: Clarendon Press, 1948

Honan, Park, Jane Austen: Her Life, New York: Fawcett Columbine, 1987

Jenkins, Elizabeth, Jane Austen, London: Gollancz, 1972

Lane, Maggie, Jane Austen's Family Through Five Generations, London: Hale, 1984

Lascelles, Mary, Jane Austen and Her Art, Oxford: Clarendon Press, 1970

Laski, Marghanita, Jane Austen and Her World, London: Thames and Hudson, 1975

Llewelyn, Margaret, Jane Austen: A Character Study, London: Kimber, 1977

Marsh, Madeleine, 'Ozias Humphry and the Austens of Sevenoaks' and 'The Portrait', Collected Reports of the Jane Austen Society, 1976–1985

Sawtell, George, 'Neither Rich nor Handsome . . .', Collected Reports of the Jane Austen Society, 1976–1985

Southam, B.C., Jane Austen's Literary Manuscripts, Oxford: Clarendon Press, 1964

Tomalin, Claire, Jane Austen: A Life, Harmondsworth: Penguin, 1997

Tucker, George Holbert, Jane Austen the Woman, London: Hale, 1994

Waldron Smithers, David, Jane Austen in Kent, Westerham: Hurtwood, 1981

Watkins, Susan, Jane Austen in Style, London: Thames and Hudson, 1997

Wilson, Margaret, Almost Another Sister, Kent Arts and Libraries, Maidstone: Kent County Council, 1990

Winchester City Council, Jane Austen's Winchester, Winchester: Winchester Museums Service, 1998

Frances Knatchbull
(Austen) Knight, George, *see* George
  Knight
(Austen) Knight, Revd William, *see*
  William Knight
Austen-Leigh, Revd James Edward, 21–2,
  34, 57–8, 63, 163, *10*

Badcock, Mr and Mrs, 40
Bagshot, Surrey, 69
Bakewell, Derbyshire, 71
Baldwin, Admiral (*Persuasion*), 116
Barne, Sarah, *see* Sarah Harding
Barne, Revd Dr Thomas, 177, 179–80
Basingstoke, Hampshire, 17–18, 27, 170
Bates, Miss (*Emma*), 114, 144
Bates, Mrs (*Emma*), 114, 144
Bath, Avon, 28, 40, 64, 67, 88, 95, 103,
  110, 116–17, 134, 145, 158–9, 163,
  166, 169, 173, 178, 184
Bather, Revd Edward, 106
Bear Hotel, Esher, Surrey, 70
Bellas, Louisa, née Lefroy, 164
Benn, Mary, 105
Benn, Mrs, 41
Bennet, Elizabeth (*Pride and Prejudice*), 23,
  69, 71, 121–5, 129, 132, 139–42,
  145–6, 161
Bennet, Jane (*Pride and Prejudice*), 42, 124,
  140
Bennet, Kitty (*Pride and Prejudice*), 139
Bennet, Lydia, *see* Lydia Wickham (*Pride
  and Prejudice*)
Bennet, Mary (*Pride and Prejudice*), 69
Bennet, Mr (*Pride and Prejudice*), 120–21,
  124–5, 132, 139
Bennet, Mrs (*Pride and Prejudice*), 63, 121,
  124–5, 132, 139–41, 146
Bentley, Hampshire, 77
Bentworth, Hampshire, 101
Benwick, Captain (*Persuasion*), 94, 135
Berlin, Germany, 76
Bertram, Edmund (*Mansfield Park*), 88,

129, 131, 146–7, 149
Bertram, Julia (*Mansfield Park*), 130
Bertram, Lady (*Mansfield Park*), 130, 134
Bertram, Maria, *see* Maria Rushworth
  (*Mansfield Park*)
Bertram, Sir Thomas (*Mansfield Park*), 130,
  135
Bifrons, Kent, 151
Bigeon, Mme, 77
Bigg, Alethea, 27, 170–73
Bigg, Catherine, *see* Catherine Hill
Bigg, Elizabeth, *see* Elizabeth Heathcote
Bigg-Wither, Anne, née Howe Frith, 173-4
Bigg-Wither, Harris, 18, 149, 171–4, 180,
  22
Bigg-Wither, Lovelace, 171
Bingley, Caroline (*Pride and Prejudice*),
  139–41
Bingley, Charles (*Pride and Prejudice*), 121,
  117, 139
Black Callerton, Northumberland, 178
Blackall, Revd Samuel, 149, 159–65, 171
Blackall, Susannah, née Lewis, 161–2
Blackall family, 164–5
Bolton, 1st Baron, 27
Bonaparte, Napoleon, 80, 159
Bond, John, 101–2, 159
Boulogne, France, 80
Bourgh, Anne de (*Pride and Prejudice*), 123
Bourgh, Lady Catherine de (*Pride and
  Prejudice*), 18, 121–4
Box Hill, Surrey, 70
Bramston, Augusta, 105
Brandon, Colonel (*Sense and Sensibility*),
  39, 129, 147–8
Brereton, Clara (*Sanditon*), 127
Brest, France, 79
Bridges, Sir Brook I, 60, 174
Bridges, Sir Brook II, 44
Bridges, Lady Dorothy, 62, 174–5
Bridges, Revd Edward, 174–6
Bridges, Lady Eleanor, née Foote, 175
Bridges, Elizabeth, *see* Elizabeth Austen

Bridges, Harriet, née Foote, 175–6
Bridges, Harriot, *see* Harriot Moore
Brighton, Sussex, 129
Brontë, Charlotte, 42, 184
Brydges, Anne, *see* Anne Lefroy
Bucklesham Hall, Suffolk, 180
Buller, Anna, 182
Buller, Revd Richard, 182
Burney, Fanny, 26

Cadell (publisher), 24, 52
Cadiz, Spain, 79
Calland, Revd John, 101
Cambridge University, 159
Campion, Jane Motley, née Austen, 47
Canopus, the, 80–81
Canterbury, Kent, 100, 108, 151, 174
Carlton House, London, 75, 176
Caroline of Brunswick, Queen, 75, 79
Cartwright, Harriet, *see* Harriet Harding Newman
Cassel, Count (*Lovers' Vows* in *Mansfield Park*), 111
Cecil, Lord David, 22, 44, 131
Chamonix, France, 165
Chandos, 1st Duke of, 19
Chapman, Dr R.W., 45, 131, 163
Chawton, Hampshire, 29–30, 33, 69, 162
Chawton Cottage (Jane Austen's house), 18, 29–30, 63, 91–3, *14, 15, 16, 17, 18*
Chawton Great House, estate and parish, 29, 62–3, 93, *13*
Cheltenham, Gloucestershire, 30, 92
Cheriton Church, Hampshire, *20*
Chilham Castle, Kent, 108
Churchill, Frank (*Emma*), 72, 114, 131–2
Chute, Revd Thomas, 27
Clacton Hall, Essex, 178
Clarke, Revd James Stanier, 75–6, 176–8
Clay, Mrs (*Persuasion*), 116, 136
Clement, Ann, 41
Cleopatra, the, 68, 84, 89
Clifton, Bristol, 161

Coburg, House of, 76, 176
Collingwood, Admiral Lord, 83
Collins, Charlotte, née Charlotte Lucas (*Pride and Prejudice*), 121–5
Collins, Mr (*Pride and Prejudice*), 121–5, 149
Combe Magna, Somerset (*Sense and Sensibility*), 128
Corunna, Spain, 34
Cowper, William, 26
Crabbe, Revd George, 26
Craven, 7th Baron, 40, 157
Crawford, Henry (*Mansfield Park*), 72, 111–12, 129–31, 135
Crawford, Mary (*Mansfield Park*), 39, 54, 146
Crawford, Mr, 167
Croft, Admiral (*Persuasion*), 82, 94
Crosby (publisher), 73
Crown Inn, Highbury (*Emma*), 69–70, 114
Cure, Mr, 68

Daedalus, the, 88
Darcy, Fitzwilliam (*Pride and Prejudice*), 71, 121–5, 139–43, 145, 153
Darcy, Georgiana (*Pride and Prejudice*), 129
Dashwood, Elinor (*Sense and Sensibility*), 23, 118–19, 128, 143, 147–8
Dashwood, John (*Sense and Sensibility*), 118
Dashwood, Marianne (*Sense and Sensibility*), 26, 39, 118–20, 127–9, 147
Dashwood, Mrs (*Sense and Sensibility*), 127–8, 147
Deal, Kent, 84–5
Deane, Basingstoke, Hampshire, 19, 54
Deane House, 87, 102, 104–5, 151
Deedes, Mrs, 41
Deedes, William, 41, 44
Denham, Sir Edward (*Sanditon*), 43, 127
Digweed, Harry, 102, 159
Digweed, Revd James, 27, 102, 159
Disney, Walt, 46
Donnington Priory, Berkshire, 180
Donwell Abbey (*Emma*), 70–71

Dorchester, 1st Baron, 27, 87
Dorchester, Lady, 87
Doyle, Sir Francis, 165
Drake, Sir Francis, 83–4
Dundas, Mr, 100
Dunwich, Suffolk, 179

East India Company, 85
East, Martha, 74
Eastwell Park, Kent, 108
Egerton, Henry, 68
Egerton, Thomas, 67
Egremont, 3rd Earl of, 177, 179
Elephant, the, 82, 84, 161
Elizabeth I, Queen, 45–6
Elliot, Anne (*Persuasion*), 23, 95, 115–17,
    136, 142–3, 145–6, 155, 182, 185
Elliot, Elizabeth (*Persuasion*), 116, 118, 142
Elliot, Mary, *see* Mary Musgrove
    (*Persuasion*)
Elliot, Sir Walter (*Persuasion*), 115–18,
    136, 142, 146
Elliot, William (*Persuasion*), 135–6, 142
Elliot, the late Lady (*Persuasion*), 115, 132
Elton, Augusta, née Hawkins (*Emma*),
    114–15, 134, 144
Elton, Mr (*Emma*), 115, 133–4, 149, 157
Endymion, the, 84
Entraigues, Comte d', 69
Esher, Surrey, 70–1
Evelina, 103
Evelyn, Mrs, 166
Evelyn, William, 40, 166
Exeter, Devon, 164
Exmouth, Devon, 179

Fairfax, Jane (*Emma*), 132, 144
Faversham, Kent, 19, 103
Ferrars, Edward (*Sense and Sensibility*), 119,
    147–9
Ferrers, Revd Edmund, 20
Feuillide, Elizabeth (Eliza) de, *see*
    Elizabeth Austen

Feuillide, Hastings de, 25, 66
Feuillide, Jean Capot, Comte de, 25, 42
Fielding, Henry, 26
Fitzhugh, Valentine, 104
Fitzwilliam, Colonel (*Pride and Prejudice*),
    139
Foote, Eleanor, *see* Eleanor Bridges
Foote, Harriet, *see* Harriet Bridges
Forster, E.M., 22
Fowle, Charles, 152, 157–9
Fowle, Fulwar, 34
Fowle, Honoria, née Townsend, 159
Fowle, Revd Thomas (father), 157
Fowle, Revd Thomas (son), 42, 152, 157,
    159
Fredville, Kent, 107
French Revolution, 25, 42, 66

Gambier, Admiral, 1st Baron, 80, 89
Gardiner, Revd Dr, 106
Gauntlett, Mr, 102
George III, King 179
George IV, King, *see* Prince Regent
Gibraltar, 80, 89
Gibson, Mary, *see* Mary Austen
Goddard, Mrs (*Emma*), 114
Godmersham Park, Kent, 19, 29, 44, 55,
    59–61, 77, 84, 86, 91, 103, 108–9, 176,
    12
Goldsmith, Oliver, 26
Goodnestone, Kent, 60, 174
Gosport, Hampshire, 29, 87, 104
Gould, Revd John, 103
Grant, Dr (*Mansfield Park*), 149
Granville, Mr, 167
Gregory family, 106
Guildford, Surrey, 69
Guillemarde, Mr, 68
Gunthorpe, William, 106

Haden, Charles, 74–5, 99–100
Halifax, Emma, 106
Halifax, Canada, 68

Hall, Elizabeth, *see* Elizabeth Harding Newman
Hall, Mr (hairdresser), 21, 47
Hall, Mr and Mrs, of Sherborne, 36
Hammond, William, 105
Hampson, Mr, later Sir Thomas, 68
Hancock, Elizabeth (Eliza), *see* Elizabeth Austen
Hancock, Philadelphia, née Austen, 25
Hanwell, Middlesex, 76
Harding, Anne Lefroy, née Sadleir, 178
Harding, Benjamin, 178
Harding, Elizabeth, 178
Harding, John (father), 179
Harding, John (son), 178–80
Harding, Sarah, née Barne, 179
Harding Newman, Anna, née Parry, 180
Harding Newman, Elizabeth, née Hall, 47–8, 180–81
Harding Newman, Harriet, née Cartwright, 180
Harding Newman, Richard, 178
Harding Newman, Thomas (father), 178–81
Harding Newman, Dr Thomas (son), 47, 179, 181
Hartfield (*Emma*), 133
Harville, Captain (*Persuasion*), 82, 94, 135, 185
Harwood, Earle, 104–5
Harwood, Mrs, 104–5
Harwood family, 104, 151–2, 158
Hastings, Warren, 25, 73, 80
Hawkins, Augusta, *see* Augusta Elton (*Emma*)
Hayter, Charles (*Persuasion*), 91
Heartley, Mr, 155–6
Heathcote, Elizabeth, née Bigg, 170
Heywood, Charlotte (*Sanditon*), 43
Highbury (*Emma*), 69–71, 114
Hill, Catherine, née Bigg, 27, 101, 170–71, 173
Hog's Back, Guildford, Surrey, 70

Holder, James, 102, 178
Holly Bush, Derbyshire, 180
Home, Sir Everard, 92
Honan, Park, 39, 153
Hornchurch, Essex, 178
Howe Frith, Anne, *see* Anne Bigg-Wither
Hubback, Catherine, née Austen, 162, 164
Hudson, Colonel, 34
Humphry, Ozias, 46
Hungerford, Berkshire, 159

Indian, the, 89
Irrawady, R., Burma, 94
Irvine, Miss, 38
Ivybridge, Devon, 179
Ixworth Abbey, Suffolk, 180

Jackson, Alicia, 106
Jackson, Eleanor, *see* Eleanor Austen
James (servant to the Austens), 110
Jenkins, Elizabeth, 56, 148
Jenner, Dr Edward, 105
Johnson, Dr Samuel, 26, 103

Kempshott Park, Hampshire, 87, 158
Kingsdown, Somerset, 166
Kingston, Surrey, 69
Kintbury, Berkshire, 157
Knatchbull, Sir Edward, 62
Knatchbull, Frances (Fanny), née (Austen) Knight, 44–5, 48, 61–3, 74–5, 99, 107–8, 181–2
Knatchbull, Wyndham, 67
Knight, Catherine, née Knatchbull, 44, 176
Knight, Edward (Austen) (Jane's brother), 19, 29–30, 44, 59–64, 74, 84, 86–7, 91, 95, 166, 174, 179, 181, 5
Knight, Edward (Austen) (Lane's nephew), 61, 63
Knight, Elizabeth, *see* Elizabeth Rice
Knight, Frances (Fanny) (Austen), *see* Frances Knatchbull

Knight, George (Austen), 60, 61, 63
Knight, Thomas (father), 19, 29, 59
Knight, Thomas (son), 29, 59
Knight, Revd William (Austen), 20, 58
Knightley, George (*Emma*), 70, 132, 143–5
Knightley, Isabella, née Woodhouse
    (*Emma*), 109, 144
Knightley, John (*Emma*), 91, 109, 144

Lambton (*Pride and Prejudice*), 71
Langlois, Benjamin, 153
Lark, the, 79
Lascelles, Mary, 94, 146, 184
Latouche, Mrs, 74
Laverstoke, Hampshire, 54
Leatherhead, Surrey, 70
Lefroy, Anna, née Austen, 41, 54–5, 57,
    63, 72, 77, 95, 106–7, 164, 178–9
Lefroy, Anne, née Brydges, 42, 87, 152–6,
    159–61, 174, 175, 178
Lefroy, Revd Benjamin, 41, 106, 178–9
Lefroy, Elizabeth, *see* Elizabeth Sadleir
Lefroy, Revd George, 154
Lefroy, Revd Isaac Peter George, 42,
    152–4, 178
Lefroy, Louisa, *see* Louisa Bellas
Lefroy, Lucy, *see* Lucy Rice
Lefroy, Mary, née Paul, 156
Lefroy, Thomas Langlois, 152–7, 160–61,
    171, 174–5, 178, *21*
Lefroy family, 178–9
Leigh, Cassandra, *see* Cassandra Austen
Leigh family, 19
Leigh Perrot, James, 19, 59
Leigh Perrot, Jane, 38, 58, 159, 166
Leopold, Prince, later King of the Belgians,
    76
Lewis, Susannah, *see* Susannah Blackall
Ligurienne, La, 80, 83
Lincoln's Inn, London, 159
Llewelyn, Margaret, 160
Lloyd, Martha, *see* Martha Austen
Lloyd, Mary, *see* Mary Austen

Loiterer, The, 54
London, 21, 29, 67, 69, 73–4, 77, 92, 123,
    153, 156, 177
London, the, 79
Lovers' Vows, 111
Lucan, 2nd Earl of, 40
Lucas, Charlotte, *see* Charlotte Collins
    (*Pride and Prejudice*)
Lucas, Sir William and Lady (*Pride and
    Prejudice*), 121
Lushington, Stephen Rumbold, 100
Lyford, John, 151
Lyford, Mrs, 106
Lyme Regis, Dorset, 26, 110, 166, 169

Maitland, the Misses, 103
Mant, Mrs, 41
Mant, Revd Dr Richard, 40–41
Manydown Park, Hampshire, 18, 27, 149,
    152, 170–73, *23*
Marcou (St Marcouf), France, 104
Marseilles, France, 80
Mary, Queen of Scots, 45
Mascall, Robert, 103
Mathew, Anne, *see* Anne Austen
Maxwell, Mr, 106
Mayow, Ursula, 165
Meryton (*Pride and Prejudice*), 129
Middleton, Sir John (*Sense and Sensibility*),
    118–19
Middleton, Lady (*Sense and Sensibility*), 118
Milton, John, 100
Mitford, Mary Russell, 22, 31, 154
Mitford, Mrs, 22
Moira, Lord, later 1st Marquess of
    Hastings, 80
Moore, Revd George, 108–9
Moore, Harriot, née Bridges, 108–9
Moore, John, Archbishop of Canterbury,
    108
Moore, General Sir John, 34–5
Morland, Catherine (*Northanger Abbey*),
    120, 146

Murray, John, 73
Musgrave, Tom (*The Watsons*), 127
Musgrove, Charles (*Persuasion*), 91
Musgrove, Mary, née Elliot (*Persuasion*),
    117

'Nameless Lover', 28, 149, 151, 162–6, 183
Napoleon, *see* Bonaparte
Napoleonic Wars, 27, 34–5, 42, 79–81,
    88–9
National Portrait Gallery, 46
Nelmes, Hornchurch, Essex, 178
Nelson, Horatio, 1st Viscount, 35, 79–81,
    83–4
Neptune, the, 80
Netherfield (*Pride and Prejudice*), 42, 69,
    121, 140
Newbury, Berkshire, 159
Newman, Cardinal John, 34, 149
Newman family, *see* Harding Newman
Nicolson, Harold, 36
Nile, Battle of the, 80
Nore, The, Kent, 84, 91
Norris, Mrs (*Mansfield Park*), 135
North Cadbury, Somerset, 161
Norton Court, Kent, 100

Ogle, Mr, 99
Overton, Hampshire, 54
Oxenden, Mary, 105
Oxford, city and county of, 20, 65
Oxford University, 54, 65, 103, 171

Pakenham, Mr, 85
Palermo, Sicily, 79
Palmer, Charlotte (*Sense and Sensibility*),
    109
Palmer, Frances (Fanny), *see* Frances
    Austen
Palmer, Harriet, *see* Harriet Austen
Palmer, John, Attorney-General of
    Bermuda, 90
Palmer, Mr (*Sense and Sensibility*), 109

Papillon, Revd John, 105, 176
Parker, Mr (*Sanditon*), 127
Parry, Anna, *see* Anna Harding Newman
Pasley, Captain Sir Charles, 149
Paul, Mary, *see* Mary Lefroy
Pearson, Mary, 25
Pemberley (*Pride and Prejudice*), 71
Percy, Mrs and daughters, 106
Peterel, the, 79
Petworth House, Sussex, 177, 179
Phillot, Venerable Dr James, 106
Phoenix, the, 92
Pilgrim, Constance, 165
Plumtre, John, 107
Portal, Benjamin, 99
Portsmouth, Earl of, 27
Portsmouth, Hampshire, 79, 84, 88, 95,
    104, 134
Powlett, Anne, née Temple, 37, 157
Powlett, Revd Charles, 155–7
Powlett, Colonel Thomas and brother, 103
Price, Fanny (*Mansfield Park*), 25–6, 80,
    88, 95, 129–31, 134–5, 146–7
Price, Mr (*Mansfield Park*), 94, 134–5
Price, Mrs (*Mansfield Park*), 44
Price, William (*Mansfield Park*), 80, 86, 88,
    94, 130–31, 134–5
Prince Regent, Prince of Wales, later King
    George IV, 75–6, 177, 179

Quidhampton, Hampshire, 174

Ramsgate, Kent, 80
Reading Abbey School, Berkshire, 20
Red House, Sevenoaks, Kent, 19
Repton, Humphrey, 112
Rice, Edward, 179
Rice, Elizabeth, née Knight, 179
Rice, Revd Henry, 105–6
Rice, John Morland, 48, 181
Rice, Lucy, née Lefroy, 179
Rice Portrait, 46–8, 179, 181, 24
Richardson, Samuel, 26

Ripley, Surrey, 69
Robinson, Revd Matthew, 105
Rosings (*Pride and Prejudice*), 122–3
Rowling, Kent, 60, 174
Rushworth, Maria, née Bertram (*Mansfield Park*), 111–12, 130–31
Rushworth, Mr (*Mansfield Park*), 111–12, 130
Rushworth, Mrs (*Mansfield Park*), 112
Russell, Lady (*Persuasion*), 142, 154–5
Russell, Revd Dr, 154

Sadleir, Anne Lefroy, see Anne Lefroy Harding
Sadleir, Elizabeth, née Lefroy, 178
St Albans, the, 35, 85
St Domingo, Battle of, 81–2
St Lawrence, Lady Frances, 106
Sawbridge, Miss, 106
Scorpion, the, 89
Scott, Sir Walter, 26, 95
Serle (*Emma*), 113
Sevenoaks, Kent, 19
Seymour, William, 68
Sharp, Anne, 44
Sheridan, Richard Brinsley, 26
Sidmouth, Devon, 26, 164, 183
Simpson, Captain, 68
Simpson, Captain (brother), 68
Smith, Harriet (*Emma*), 133–4, 144
Smith, Mrs (*Persuasion*), 117
Sondes, Lady, 37
Sotherton Court (*Mansfield Park*), 112
Sotterley, Suffolk, 179
Southam, Brian, 66, 177
Southampton, Hampshire, 28, 56, 61, 81
Southey, Robert, 84
Speen, Berkshire, 180
Spencer, 2nd Earl, 80
Spicer, Mr, 70
Spitswick, Devon, 179
Stanhope, Admiral Henry, 103
Stanhope, Lady Hester, 35

Steele, Anne (*Sense and Sensibility*), 118–19
Steele, Lucy (*Sense and Sensibility*), 118–19
Steventon Manor, Hampshire, 102
Steventon Rectory and Parish, 19, 20, 22, 27–9, 54, 56–7, 77, 87, 102, 104–5, 11
Stoneleigh Abbey, Warwickshire, 19
Sunninghill, Surrey, 76
Susan, Lady see Lady Susan Vernon (*Lady Susan*)

Taylor, Edward, 108
Taylor, Elizabeth, *see* Elizabeth Harding
Temple, Anne, *see* Anne Powlett
Terry, Patience, 105
Terry, Stephen, 27
Thackeray, William Makepeace, 148
Thorpe, Isabella (*Northanger Abbey*), 24
Thorpe, John (*Northanger Abbey*), 120–21
Thrush, the, (*Mansfield Park*), 134–5
Tilney, Eleanor (*Northanger Abbey*), 146, 158
Tilney, Frederick (*Northanger Abbey*), 24, 146
Tilney, General (*Northanger Abbey*), 146
Tilney, Henry (*Northanger Abbey*), 24, 72, 120, 145–6, 149, 158
Tilson, Frances, 41
Torquay, Devon, 179
Totnes, Devon, 164
Townsend, Honoria, *see* Honoria Fowle
Trafalgar, Battle of, 80, 83–4, 89
Tucker, George Holbert, 165
Trinity College, Dublin, 152–3
Tunbridge Wells, Kent, 77
Twisleton, Hon. Mary, 40, 166

Unicorn, the, 88

Vanity Fair, 148
Vernon, Lady Susan (*Lady Susan*), 66
Victoria, Queen, 76
Villeneuve, Admiral Pierre de, 81

Walcot Church, Bath, Avon, 178
Wales, Prince of, later King George IV, *see*
    Prince Regent
Waller, Richard and wife, 35–6
Wallis, Colonel (*Persuasion*), 117
Walter, Henry, 68
Walter, Philadelphia, *see* Philadelphia
    Whitaker
Warren, John Willing, 151, 155–6
Watkins, Charles, 151
Wentworth, Captain Frederick
    (*Persuasion*), 82, 86, 94, 116, 135,
    142–3, 145, 165, 185
Westminster Abbey, London, 75
Weston, Anne, née Taylor (*Emma*), 72,
    144
Weston, Mr (*Emma*), 72, 132, 144
Weston Green, Esher, Surrey, 70
Whitaker, Philadelphia, née Walter, 24, 66
Wickham, George (*Pride and Prejudice*),
    124, 127, 129
Wickham, Lydia, née Bennet (*Pride and
    Prejudice*), 22–3, 124–5, 129, 139
Widley, Hampshire, 170
Wigram, Henry, 77
Wildman, Mr, 108
William IV, King, 179
Williams, Lady Jane, née Cooper, 42
Willoughby, John (*Sense and Sensibility*),
    119–20, 127–9
Winchester, Hampshire, 29
Winchester Cathedral, Winchester,
    Hampshire, 170
Winchester College, Winchester,
    Hampshire, 34, 57
Wither family, 170
Woodhouse, Emma (*Emma*) 18, 59, 69, 72,
    109, 112–13, 132–4, 143–6
Woodhouse, Isabella, *see* Isabella Knightley
    (*Emma*)
Woodhouse, Mr (*Emma*), 112–15, 144, 146
Woodhouse, the late Mrs (*Emma*), 113,
    132

Wootton St Lawrence, Hampshire, 170
Wordsworth, John, 165
Wordsworth, William, 165
Wortley-Montagu, Lady Mary, 23
Wye, R., Herefordshire, 162
Wylmot, Mrs, 40
Wymering, Hampshire, 170

Zoffany, Johann, 46, 181